Famous Court Cases That Became Movies

THE AMISTAD MUTINY

From the **Court Case** to the **Movie**

Melissa Eisen Azarian

Enslow Publishers, Inc.
40 Industrial Road
Box 398
Berkeley Heights, NJ 07922
USA

http://www.enslow.com

This book is dedicated to my parents, Harold and Peggy Eisen.

Author's Note

In connection with his purchase of Sengbe Pieh, Jose Ruiz secured false papers that identified Sengbe as Joseph Cinquez. Though the slave owners were being deceptive, at that time the Mende language did not have a written form. Thus, a correct spelling of Sengbe Pieh did not exist. Publications refer to him as Jingua, Cinquez, Sengbe, and, most often, Cinque. After learning English, Sengbe wrote letters bearing the signature "Cinque," suggesting that he adopted this name while in America. This book will refer to him as Cinque in most instances.

Copyright © 2009 by Melissa Eisen Azarian

Library of Congress Cataloging-in-Publication Data

Azarian, Melissa Eisen.
    The Amistad mutiny : from the court case to the movie / Melissa Eisen Azarian.
       p. cm. — (Famous court cases that became movies)
    Includes bibliographical references and index.
    Summary: "Explores the mutiny aboard the Amistad, including the slave revolt onboard, the trial
       of the slaves in U.S. courts, the appeal to the Supreme Court, and the inspiration for the
       movie, Amistad"—Provided by publisher.
    ISBN-13: 978-0-7660-3054-1
    ISBN-10: 0-7660-3054-7
      1. Cinque—Trials, litigation, etc.—Juvenile literature. 2. Trials (Mutiny)—United States—
Juvenile literature. 3. Fugitive slaves—Legal status, laws, etc.—United States—Juvenile literature.
4. Amistad (Schooner)—Juvenile literature. 5. Slave trade—America—History—Juvenile
literature. 6. Slave insurrections—United States—Juvenile literature. 7. Antislavery
movements—United States—Juvenile literature. I. Title.
    KF223.C56A93 2010
    326.0973'09034—dc22

            2008044581

Printed in the United States of America

10 9 8 7 6 5 4 3 2 1

To Our Readers:
We have done our best to make sure all Internet Addresses in this book were active and appropriate when we went to press. However, the author and the publisher have no control over and assume no liability for the material available on those Internet sites or on other Web sites they may link to. Any comments or suggestions can be sent by e-mail to comments@enslow.com or to the address on the back cover.

♻ Enslow Publishers, Inc., is committed to printing our books on recycled paper. The paper in every book contains 10% to 30% post-consumer waste (PCW). The cover board on the outside of each book contains 100% PCW. Our goal is to do our part to help young people and the environment too!

Illustration Credits: Courtesy of Melissa Eisen Azarian, pp. 106, 109; Enslow Publishers, Inc., p. 11; Everett Collection, pp. 1, 86, 91, 96, 100; Library of Congress, pp. 9, 14, 17, 22, 25, 35, 39, 42, 47, 56, 64, 72, 76, 83; The New Haven Museum & Historical Society, pp. 4, 29, 63.

Cover Illustrations: Courthouse logo—Artville; gavel—Digital Stock; movie still from *Amistad*—Everett Collection.

CONTENTS

A portrait of Cinque, painted by Nathaniel Jocelyn while the *Amistad* Africans awaited trial.

Chapter 1

Cinque's Story

All hail! thou truly noble chief,
Who scorned to live a cowering slave;
Thy name shall stand on history's leaf;
Amid the mighty and the brave.

—Excerpted from "To Cinque," by James Monroe Whitfield, in *America and Other Poems* (Buffalo, 1853)

New Haven, Connecticut, January 1840. Everyone in the courtroom had been waiting for this moment. It was Cinque's turn to speak. A peaceful farmer, Cinque had been abducted into slavery in his native Africa one year earlier. Months later, he led a deadly mutiny on the *Amistad*, a schooner transporting fifty-three Africans from Havana to Puerto Principe, Cuba.

Following the revolt, the *Amistad* Africans yearned to go back home. But they lacked navigational skills. They depended on two Spaniards aboard to steer them in the right direction. The Spaniards purposely steered away from Africa. The *Amistad* wound up in New York. Soon jailed in Connecticut, the Africans faced a trial for their lives.

The case exposed Cuba's widespread violation of a ban on slave trading. Because Cuba was a Spanish colony, Spain wanted to quiet any discussion of these unlawful activities. The Spanish minister in Washington, Angel Calderón de la Barca, pressed for the immediate surrender of the *Amistad* and its cargo to the Spanish government. He wanted the Africans to be returned to Cuba to stand trial on charges of piracy and murder. If returned, the Africans would have been executed or reenslaved.

Like Spain, President Martin Van Buren hoped for a speedy resolution. In the middle of a reelection campaign, Van Buren did not dare to anger voters in the slave-owning South. His advisers recommended backing Spain's demand. They thought that if the Africans left the United States, the matter would be out of the headlines and public discourse.

While some Northerners felt that the Africans were entitled to freedom, many Southerners believed that the Africans would be better off as slaves. Despite racial prejudice throughout the United States, growing sentiment in the North was against enslavement as inhumane. Most Northern states had already outlawed slavery or at least pushed it to extinction. However, the Southern economy largely depended on it. The issue of slavery threatened to divide the country; there were murmurs about an inevitable civil war.

Abolitionists Find A Hero

Some of the *Amistad* Africans bundled up and walked through New Haven to the courthouse on January 8 to hear Cinque's testimony.

Most onlookers in the trial court sided with the Africans. Among them were many women, religious leaders, and Yale students of religion and law, whose classes had been called off to enable them to observe the proceedings. Not a seat was empty. Those who found a place remained sitting during court breaks, because they did not want to lose their spots.

The courtroom was full of attorneys, including the Africans' lawyers and the U.S. district attorney for Connecticut. Parties seeking a financial reward for finding the wayward slave ship had representation in court as well.

District Judge Andrew Judson claimed to be anti-slavery. Yet he had earlier fought against a school for black girls in his town. He also opposed abolitionists, people who believed that the sale and ownership of human beings was wrong.

Abolitionists wanted to end slavery. They seized any opportunity to attract national coverage and sympathy for slaves. The *Amistad* case gave them a perfect opportunity to keep the public microscope on slavery. Cinque was the ideal hero.

Cinque quickly achieved celebrity status in the United States. Publications glorified him as a rare spirit who possessed courage and was "accustomed to command."[1] Street vendors sold prints of him. People compared him to heroes of ancient Greece and Rome. Inaccurate reports circulated that he had been a slave trader with three wives.[2] A Southern newspaper labeled Cinque a "black piratical murderer."[3] The publicity created an exciting aura around Cinque, building anticipation for his testimony.

When Cinque rose to testify, he had a commanding presence. At nearly 5 feet 8 inches, he was taller than most people from Mende, a part of Sierra Leone on the west coast of Africa. He looked regal, wrapped in a blanket because he was unaccustomed to the climate of Connecticut in January. Spectators listened with "breathless attention" as Cinque spoke.[4] His was the story of the inhumanity inflicted on millions of Africans forced into slavery.

From Freedom to Bondage

Before he was known as Cinque, he was Sengbe Pieh, a freeborn rice planter in the African farming village of Mende. He and his wife lived in a cone-shaped hut with their son, two daughters, and Sengbe's father.

As he headed to his fields one January morning in 1839, four men captured Sengbe, then twenty-five years old. They tied Sengbe's right hand to his neck and made him walk to a nearby village in the Vai region. There, they brought him to Mayagilalo, the man who had ordered them to abduct a person like Sengbe.

Tribal law in Africa dictated that debts be paid, or the debtor would go into slavery. Sengbe thought he might have forgotten to pay back money to someone. But Sengbe's days as a peaceful farmer may have ended

A portrait of Cinque by James Sheffield that appeared in the New York *Sun* on August 31, 1839.

because Mayagilalo owed money to an African king's son. Either way, Sengbe was used to settle a debt.

After a month in Vai country, Sengbe and other captives were marched to Lomboko. Off the west coast of Africa, Lomboko was a slave-trading island controlled by Don Pedro Blanco. When Blanco first came to the region as the captain of a slave ship in 1824, not many slaves were available. Blanco was an opportunist. He built an empire by providing a central location for slave captains to purchase humans.[5]

The captives at Lomboko were tightly packed into barracoons. These were holding pens, oblong structures with thatched roofs of grass. The barracoons had open walls with prison-like bars.

Every day, more Africans were thrown into the barracoons, each with similar stories about being kidnapped. Most were men: farmers, hunters, and blacksmiths. But women and children joined them too. They had been taken from their homes in the middle of the night or while walking in daytime. Several had been slaves for years and were at Lomboko to be resold. One was traded by his uncle for a coat. Another survived a bloody battle in his village, only to be captured and condemned to slavery. A few men were abducted after being caught with another man's wife; the penalty for that behavior was enslavement.

In the barracoons, the captives ate rice, oil, and sometimes fish, fruit, or vegetables. For sales purposes, the traders needed the Africans to appear healthy and nourished. Sengbe spent two months at Lomboko, until a day in April 1839 when the slave ship arrived.

Triangular Trade

Slavery operated on a triangular trade system. This meant that there were three journeys. The first part was the outward journey, in which goods manufactured in Europe were traded for slaves in Africa. The next phase was the middle passage. During the middle passage, slaves were brought from Africa to Brazil, the Caribbean, and the Americas, where they were exchanged for sugar. Finally, on the homeward passage, sugar and other goods were brought back to Europe and sold for cash.

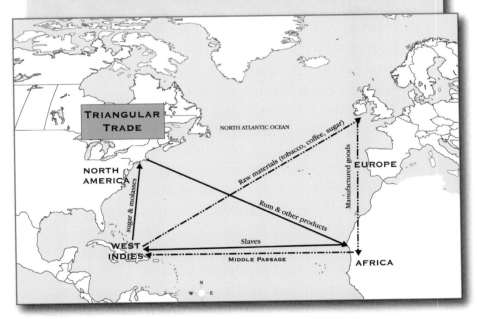

The Middle Passage

Along with Sengbe, more than five hundred Africans were sold that day, and then corralled onto the *Tecora*, the Portuguese slaver that carried them to Cuba. They had to board quickly before daybreak, to avoid being sighted by a British cruiser. In 1807, Parliament had abolished the slave trade in the British Empire. British ships patrolled the empire's waters to enforce the ban.

The Africans were shoved into large canoes, which brought them to the ship. They began the "Middle Passage." According to one account, during the three-month journey, the Africans "endured all the horrors of a prison combined with those of crossing the ocean in an old-time sailing craft."[6]

At the outset, slaves were stripped naked. They were sent into the slave holds, never high enough for people to stand upright. On many ships the space was less than 3 feet high.[7] Roomier than most, the slave decks on the *Tecora* were close to four feet tall.

Slave ships were long and low. They were low to escape the notice of British warships. They were long to carry large numbers of Africans. Some captains believed in "tight packing," or jamming as many slaves as possible into the holds. These captains figured that the number of survivors would compensate for the unavoidable fatalities from overcrowded conditions. Other captains preferred to give slaves enough room, increasing everyone's chances for survival.[8]

Sometimes males and females were placed in separate areas. The reason for the separation was that the women were "usually regarded as fair prey for the sailors."[9] Another reason for separating them was the fear that if they were kept together, the women might encourage the men to revolt.[10] The men were strong and they outnumbered the crew. Rebellions occurred with some frequency on the coast at the beginning of the journey, when slaves still had the strength to plan a mutiny.[11]

Women and children, who were not considered a threat to the crew's safety, were not usually in chains. The men wore heavy iron collars, so that they could be linked by their necks. For the entire voyage, the men were chained together, normally in pairs, by the wrists and legs. The manacles made it difficult to move independently. They also caused wounds. In a further act of cruelty, the ship's crew would rub vinegar and gunpowder into these gashes.

The slave holds were hot, with little ventilation. The latrines were buckets, often inaccessible, so people stewed in their own bodily waste. The area reeked of sweat and other noxious odors. Diseases such as malaria, scurvy, and smallpox raged in the unsanitary conditions. On the *Tecora*, some captives contracted dysentery, then known as the "bloody flux."[12] A surgeon on another slave ship described the floor of the slave hold as being "so covered with blood and mucus . . . that it resembled a slaughterhouse."[13]

Other ailments were prevalent, like seasickness, dehydration, and contagious eye infections resulting in blindness. The ships were prone to rat and lice infestation. Captives were subject to beatings.

Slaves were brought onto the deck in small groups if the ship's physician felt that they needed fresh air.

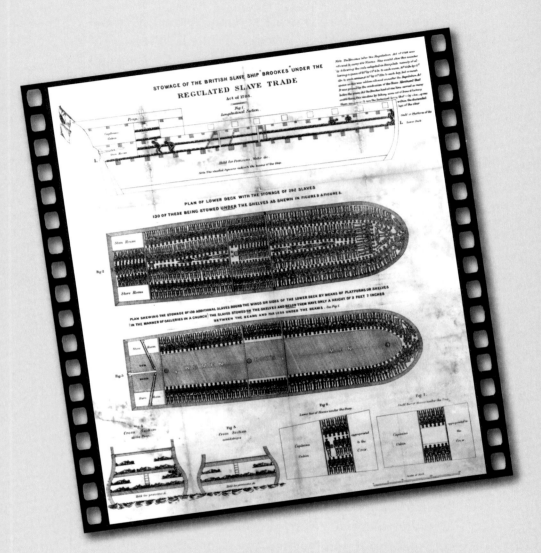

A diagram of a slave ship shows how people were crammed together into incredibly tight spaces for the trip across the Atlantic Ocean.

The crew shouted commands in a language the Africans could not speak. They would order the Africans—still chained together—to dance, a marketing tool to keep the slaves in decent physical condition for sale. In bad weather, or at times when there was a risk of being sighted by a warship, captives had to remain below.

Slaves ate twice a day, dunking their hands in buckets of rice, yams, or beans. Meals were supervised. Those who attempted self-starvation were beaten or force-fed, often to the point of vomiting. Crew members could make slaves eat by using a "speculum oris," a scissors-like instrument that would force the jaws open.

Supplies began to dwindle toward the end of most voyages. Food and water often had to be rationed. Although there was plenty of rice on the *Tecora*, there was not enough water.[14]

On all slave ships, the Middle Passage was so unbearable that it provoked suicidal thoughts. Before boarding, some Africans, who perhaps had never seen the ocean, tried self-strangulation or drowning. Netting along the side of the upper decks prevented people from committing suicide by jumping overboard.[15] It also kept British naval officers from boarding slave ships in groups.[16]

The Middle Passage always resulted in deaths. The *Tecora* was no exception. A slaver could lose one third of the human cargo from disease. Those who survived were gaunt and filthy. Some Africans entered a catatonic state of shock called "fixed melancholy." They died from complete despair.[17] The dead were tossed overboard.

During the last few days of the journey, the bustle of activity hinted that the trip would soon be over. On the captain's orders, the crew unchained most of the slaves and brought them on deck to be bathed. The captives would be given clean clothing and larger portions of food and water if there were adequate provisions.

Reaching Land

The *Tecora* anchored soon after sighting land.[18] After two months at sea, the slaves had to wait until nighttime to disembark to avoid capture by a British warship. Once they arrived at an isolated point on Cuba's shore, the blacks were hastened into small boats. From the beach, they walked three miles through the jungle until they reached warehouses, where they spent two weeks recovering. Then, one June night, they were marched again. They spent daylight locked in barracoons at the slave market.

Late in June, slave traders Jose Ruiz and Pedro Montes arrived at the barracoons. Not surprisingly, slave traders even practiced deception against each other. When a slave became useless because of illness, the master would send the ailing slave to brokers.[19] The dealer would inject mineral drugs into the slaves to bloat their flesh, and give them stimulants to add luster to their skin.[20] Experienced traders could detect such trickery, by looking at the yellow eyes, swollen tongues, and feverish skin.[21]

Ruiz knew the slave business. He selected his purchases and made them stand in a row:

> He looked in their eyes, opened their mouths, and checked their nostrils. He examined them for venereal disease and anal problems. He thumped them and thwacked them with the practice of long experience of a man dealing in human flesh.[22]

Captives being transported through the interior of Africa to the coast by Portuguese slave traders.

Amistad: The Movie

More than one hundred and fifty years after Cinque led the revolt, DreamWorks SKG released *Amistad*, directed by Steven Spielberg. The 1997 movie, which had a number of historical inaccuracies, received mixed reviews. It was often compared unfavorably to Spielberg's more critically acclaimed and commercially successful film, *Schindler's List*.

In the *San Francisco Chronicle*, critic Edward Guthmann wrote: "An admirable but disappointing effort, Spielberg uses a more conventional format than he did in the stripped-down black-and-white, *Schindler's List*, and delivers a film that veers between stoic political correctness and mushy pop-Hollywood platitudes."[23]

Nonetheless, *Amistad* succeeded in promoting public knowledge of the incident. As Stanley Kauffman wrote in *The New Republic*: "*Amistad*, shortcomings and all, is solid, engrossing. While it's in progress, it envelops us; paradoxically, when it's finished, it seems to stand free, like a strong sculpture."[24]

Forty-nine men passed Ruiz's inspection. Ruiz paid $450 for each of them, including Sengbe Pieh. Montes bought four children, three girls and a boy.

The purchases violated a treaty, which took effect in 1820, outlawing the slave trade in Spanish territories. Even though importing slaves was illegal, those who had been living in Cuba before 1820 were still lawfully enslaved. *Ladinos* is the word for slaves who were born in Cuba or resided there earlier than 1820. *Bozales* were recently imported Africans who could not be traded or transported.

Slave traders knew how to get around the law with bribes. The governor of Havana accepted "hush money" of ten or fifteen dollars per slave who arrived at the port.[25] Within a few days of purchasing Sengbe and the other Africans, Ruiz and Montes paid the fee at the governor's office for *traspassos*. These documents authorized the transport of slaves to another part of the island. Because *bozales* were illegal, *traspassos* would falsely indicate that the slaves were *ladinos*.

To add believability to the *traspasso*'s assertion that a person was a *ladino*, slave purchasers would often change African names to ones that sounded Spanish. This is how Sengbe Pieh became Joseph Cinquez and, later, "Cinque."

After Ruiz and Montes took care of these formalities, the naked captives were given loincloths and a meal. They marched again in darkness through Havana, the men in chains and iron collars. Cinque had endured captivity for nearly six months. Like the other Africans, all he wanted was to go home.

Chapter 2

The Mutiny

After marching in darkness, Ruiz, Montes, and the Africans boarded a schooner. The name painted on it was *La Amistad*, Spanish for "friendship." The Africans were sent into its hold. Onboard the *Amistad* were Ramon Ferrer, the captain and owner; two sailors; and the captain's slaves—Antonio, a sixteen-year-old cabin boy, and Celestino, the biracial cook. The schooner carried $250 in cash, along with cargo and provisions valued at $40,000.

Early in the trip, Ruiz and Montes conferred with Captain Ferrer. They decided against chaining the captives in the hold, even though the African adults outnumbered the crew, forty-nine to seven. They did not expect any trouble on the short sail to their destination of Puerto Principe, Cuba.

On the second day of travel, a change in the winds meant that the voyage would last longer than the usual two days. Food and water had to be rationed. Tempers began to flare under the tropical sun. A crew member beat Burnah, one of the captives, for trying to take more than the daily allotment of a half cup of water.

Ruiz and Montes permitted a few Africans at a time to come up for fresh air. Once, when he was on deck, Cinque used sign language to ask Celestino what was going to happen to the Africans. The cook made a fatal joke: Celestino grinned and pointed to barrels of beef across the room and then to an empty one behind him. He indicated with his fingers that upon arrival in Puerto Principe, the Spaniards planned to slit all of the slaves' throats, chop their bodies into pieces, salt them down, and eat them as dried meat.[1]

Cinque was not being gullible for believing that the Spaniards would chop up and eat the captives. Many Africans believed tales that white people were cannibals.

Although Cinque was locked in the hold with people who did not speak the Mende language, he came across others who did. They plotted a mutiny. A young boy, Kinna, later recalled that Cinque said, "If we do nothing, we be killed. We may as well die in trying to be free as to be killed and eaten."[2]

Cinque found a nail on the deck and he hid it under his arm. Later, he used the nail to pick the lock of the iron collar around his neck.

A drawing of the slave ship *Wildfire*, made in 1860, shows the horrific conditions endured by the captives.

Grabeau, a fellow captive, helped Cinque to prepare for the rebellion. Using the same nail, they unchained the others, and searched for weapons in the boxes of cargo. They found sugar cane knives. These are used like hatchets, with one-inch thick steel handles and two-foot long blades that widen toward the end.[3]

At about 4:00 A.M. on July 2, under a stormy black sky, the Africans snuck up to the deck where Captain Ferrer slept on a mattress. Armed with knives, they surrounded Ferrer. Ruiz and Montes came running because they heard loud noises and cries of "Murder!" The captain screamed to Ruiz and Montes, "Throw some bread at them!" Cinque struck the captain with his heavy steel blade, and left the others to strangle Ferrer. Before he died, Ferrer killed one African and wounded two others with his dagger.

The Africans then headed to Celestino, the cook whose joke had prompted the revolt. They stabbed him to death.

Ruiz and Montes attempted to stop the mutiny. One of the sailors yelled, "Kill them all!" Montes slashed a few of them with his knife. Ruiz, who at twenty-four was younger than some of the Africans, ordered the mutineers back into the hold. Montes drove others behind the foresail, but the Africans wounded him in the process. Montes got into a tug-of-war over an oar. The Africans won, and began pounding him with the oar. A sailor beseeched them to spare the life of Montes, who was fifty-eight years old. When Montes bent to retrieve his weapon, an African hit him in the head with a cane knife, making a gash above his ear and knocking him down. He stumbled down to the hold, and hid under an old sail.

Ruiz surrendered with only minor injuries. Antonio, the cabin boy, was tied to an anchor, so he could not escape. The two crew members fled. Their fate remains unknown. It is presumed that they jumped overboard and drowned.

The mutiny only took a few minutes, and now Cinque, Grabeau, and Burnah were in command. At daybreak, they started searching for Montes. Cinque pulled the cover off of Montes's hiding spot. Montes pleaded for mercy as Cinque stood over him with a raised cane knife. Burnah grabbed Cinque and convinced him not to kill Montes.

The Africans did not know how to navigate a schooner. They spared Montes and Ruiz so that the Spaniards could guide them toward Africa. The Spaniards devised a secret plan, in which Montes would steer in the proper direction during the day but turn northward at night. Ruiz and Montes hoped that a British antislave patrol cruiser would rescue them.

The deceptive navigation sent the *Amistad* on a meandering path, first toward the Bahamas, and then up the east coast of the United States. They traveled in windy weather, which damaged the sails. Provisions were becoming depleted. Cinque suspected they were heading back to Havana, so he called a meeting with the other Africans. They decided to kill the two Spaniards. With dagger in hand, Cinque advanced toward Montes, but once again he spared Montes' life. Instead, Cinque stationed one of the Africans at the masthead with Montes for the rest of the trip.[4]

A drawing of the *Amistad* mutiny, showing the death of Captain Ferrer.

Their situation grew worse. Cinque had to ration food and water. When any ship approached the *Amistad*, Cinque hovered next to Ruiz and glared at him.[5] Cinque would not allow Ruiz, the only English-speaking person onboard, to talk to people on other boats.

Thirsty and desperate, some of the Africans drank saltwater or bottles of medicine that they found.[6] This made some ill and killed others. Ten Africans died on the *Amistad* from either wounds or sickness. By mid-August, the mood was grim.

Mysterious Schooner

WEIRD SHIP, one headline declared.[7] In August 1839, Americans became excited as word spread about a mysterious vessel. For about two weeks, it floated aimlessly off the east coast of the United States. The long, low black schooner had an eagle on her bow,

The Spaniards devised a secret plan, in which Montes would steer in the proper direction during the day but turn northward at night.

tattered sails, and no flag. The state of disrepair made it obvious that the schooner had been at sea for several months.

Newspapers reported many sightings and interactions with the vessel. In some instances, other boats gave the men on the schooner provisions such as apples.[8] Whenever someone from another vessel boarded, the black crew ordered the few white passengers to go below.[9] The blacks held cane knives, scaring away most help.

The blacks onboard were nearly naked. Some were wrapped in blankets.[10] Others had gold doubloons around their waists. While alongside the schooner, the captain of the *Emmeline* learned that the *Amistad* carried about three tons of money, a large amount of linen, and boxes of clothing.[11] Despite the valuables, men indicated in sign language that they were starving and out of water.

The *Emmeline* took the schooner in tow, but cast her off. It appeared that the armed black men intended to take possession of the *Emmeline*. The *Emmeline*'s captain described the crew as having a "very savage appearance," and reported that the white man who seemed to be the captain "had a piratical look" with a large moustache.[12]

In an otherwise boring summer for news—except for sporadic conflict with Indians on the frontier—the suspicious schooner stirred imaginations.[13] Was this a pirate ship? It seemed unlikely, because pirates had not terrorized the North Atlantic in years.[14] Some wondered whether it was a slaver. This also seemed improbable. Slavers had stopped traveling through Northeastern coastal waters since the outlawing of the slave trade in the United States in 1808.

News reached the United States that slaves had taken possession of a Spanish slave ship that had departed from Havana about six weeks earlier. It was undoubtedly the suspicious schooner, now drifting in New York waters.[15]

Between August 15 and 24, the Africans, desperate for provisions, dropped anchor about thirty times at different spots on the coast.[16] On August 25, they anchored off Culloden Point, at the eastern tip of Long Island, near Montauk, New York. They were unaware that New York was a free state, meaning slavery was illegal there.

Going Ashore

A group of the Africans went ashore. Naked or draped only in blankets, they wandered among the houses looking for water and other provisions. Bartering with gold doubloons from the ship, they purchased two dogs, among other items.[17]

The next day, sea captains Henry Green, Peletiah Fordham, and a few of their friends encountered the Africans on Long Island. Communicating through gestures, the Africans wanted to know if this country held slaves and if there were any Spaniards here. When Green conveyed that "it was a free country," Cinque whistled and waved his hand above his head.[18] Other Africans ran from the beach. They all jumped up and down and shouted for joy.[19] Cinque handed over his weapons to make their peaceful intentions known. Burnah, who spoke a bit of English, communicated that the Africans would give the seamen gold in exchange for returning them to Sierra Leone. Captain Green led the Africans to believe that he would take them home the next day.

In the meantime, the Navy had sent out several cutters and vessels in search of the mysterious vessel with tattered sails. The USS *Washington*, a coastal survey brig, happened to be patrolling Long Island on August 26. Lt. Richard W. Meade, aboard the *Washington*, spotted the *Amistad*, which appeared to be in distress.

On orders from Lt. Thomas Gedney, the *Washington*'s commander, Meade boarded the *Amistad*. He saw men armed with cane knives. The Spaniards came up to Meade. Montes was sobbing. Ruiz could speak English and Meade could speak Spanish. Ruiz told Meade about the mutiny.

While Ruiz was talking, Cinque came up from below, clad only in a gold necklace. Cinque leaped off the boat and swam away. After swimming for nearly a half hour, Cinque threw the necklace into the ocean and allowed the pursuers from the *Washington* to catch him. Crew members brought Cinque back to the *Amistad*. Onboard, Cinque made speeches that roused the Africans. He was put in handcuffs and kept separate from the others.

This painting shows the *Amistad*, with tattered sails, off the coast of New York. In the foreground, Africans are bargaining for supplies with people on shore.

Seizure of the *Amistad*

Gedney ordered the seizure of the schooner, the cargo, and the Africans. He towed the *Amistad* to New London, Connecticut. Slavery opponents believed that Gedney took the schooner to Connecticut because slavery was legal there, unlike New York.

In New London, Gedney contacted Norris Willcox, the U.S. marshal in New Haven, to request a district court hearing. Gedney and his crew intended to file a salvage claim, seeking a reward for rescuing the *Amistad*. If granted, the reward would be a percentage of the schooner and its cargo, estimated at $40,000, and at least $20,000 more for the human cargo. Gedney's claim fell under admiralty law, which governs legal issues arising in navigable waters.

The case raised possible federal questions. Montes and Ruiz made complaints of murder and piracy against Cinque and his fellow mutineers. William S. Holabird, U.S. district attorney in Connecticut, ordered a judicial hearing to determine whether a crime had occurred on the *Amistad*, and if so, who committed it? Holabird was likewise unsure whether a U.S. court would have jurisdiction, or the authority to hear this case, for an alleged crime which occurred on the high seas rather than on American soil.

On August 29, Andrew T. Judson, federal district judge of Connecticut, conducted an investigation aboard the *Washington* in New London harbor. The surviving *Amistad* Africans were present. Cinque wore a red flannel shirt, white pantaloons, manacles, and a calm expression. He smiled and made gestures to his throat, indicating that he believed he would be hung. No attorney appeared on behalf of the Africans, and the judge did not communicate with them.

Judson heard testimony from Meade, Ruiz, Montes, and the deceased captain's slave, Antonio. After inspecting the papers on the *Amistad*, Judson found that the documents supported the Spaniards' version of events about the mutiny. He considered the blacks to be *ladinos* who belonged to Ruiz and Montes.

The Spaniards asked the judge to deliver the schooner, its cargo, and the blacks to the Spanish consul in Boston. All of this property was theirs, he said. The judge referred the criminal case to the circuit court, and the salvage case to the district court, both to be heard in September. Judson ordered Willcox to put the blacks in custody at the New Haven jail. Willcox noted that none of the blacks responded to the Spanish names on their passports.

A grand jury would later vote on whether to indict, or formally charge, the Africans for the alleged crimes.

Chapter 3

Abolitionists Unite

By 1839, slavery was a longtime institution in America. African slaves came to Spanish Florida in the 1500s. White indentured servants from England, Ireland, and Scotland were brought to the colonies in the 1600s. They worked alongside Africans, under equally inhumane conditions.[1]

Because of increased traffic from slave ships by the 1690s, wealthy planters began to purchase African slaves instead of white servants.[2] Racism evolved as slavery grew to be more racially based. Eventually, black slave labor fueled the Southern economy.

Over fifty years before the *Amistad* case, slavery was generating controversy in the United States. At the Constitutional Convention in 1787, supporters demanded provisions acknowledging slavery. Opponents believed that the ownership of human beings conflicted with the nation's founding principles of equality and liberty. They did not want the word "slavery" to appear in this document.

To preserve the union, the founders reached a compromise. The Constitution includes three clauses that recognize slavery, without using that word. For example, one paragraph refers to "free Persons" and "all other Persons," indicating that some people were not free.

States were left to decide whether to allow slavery. Some Constitutional provisions gave incentives for expanding the number of slaves, like gaining congressional seats and power in presidential elections. However, the Constitution allowed for the end of the slave trade after twenty years—by 1807—but not until that time.

> **Opponents of slavery believed that the ownership of human beings conflicted with the nation's founding principles of equality and liberty.**

Although the law abolished the slave trade, effective in 1808, it did not abolish slavery itself. As in Cuba, no new slaves could be brought into the country, but slaves who already lived in the United States could be traded. In fact, American slaves could be sold at any moment and ripped away from their families forever. Between 1820 and 1850, the American slave market was booming.

Abolitionist Movements

For many years, religious groups in England and in the United States criticized the inhumanity of slavery. Traders ignored these calls to conscience, focusing only on the profits that slavery brought. Over time, people experienced a moral awakening. Disdain for slavery slowly replaced centuries of indifference. Organized movements on both sides of the Atlantic Ocean facilitated this shift in thought.

In America, Quakers and Baptists initiated antislavery discourse. The first antislavery society formed in Philadelphia in 1775. By the 1780s, similar organizations attracted people from urban society, such as merchants and craftsmen. They launched educational efforts to support gradual emancipation. In England, politicians led a campaign against the slave trade. Antislavery literature spread. Local abolition groups formed with connections to France, Philadelphia, and New York. Abolition became an international cause.

Abolitionists naively thought the trade would end upon the passage of the 1807 abolition acts. The opposite occurred. Over the next half century, it escalated. Cuba needed a constant stream of slaves, because it became the leading producer of sugar in the Caribbean. Cotton plantations also relied on a steady supply of slave labor. Europeans demanded more plantation products, such as coffee, tobacco, molasses, chocolate, rum, and

A newspaper classified advertisement
from the 1780s for the sale of slaves.

rice. Slaves were smuggled from Africa and Cuba to work for Southern planters.

To enforce the Abolition Act, England established a West African antislavery squadron. Patrolling 3,000 miles of coast was difficult. Parliament adopted regulations to improve conditions on slave ships, but traders routinely ignored these regulations. "Ordinary lying" was the most frequent means for disobeying the rules.[3] Slave captains maintained two logs. One was authentic for the ship's owners; the second was fraudulent, to be shown to any British officer who boarded the ship.[4] Ending the slave trade would require that other countries enact legislation similar to the American and British laws.[5]

Between 1817 and 1831, England negotiated treaties with some European countries, enabling the British to search their vessels on the high seas. But the law was confusing and ever-changing. Portuguese and Spanish vessels could not be searched at certain latitudes. American ships could never be searched. Upon sighting a British cruiser, a slave ship could hoist the flag of another nation (usually the U.S. flag) to evade capture. Slavers bypassed the laws in other ways, including carrying documents provided by the American consul in Havana, which falsely indicated that a ship had American nationality.

British naval officers were only authorized to detain vessels "on the single and simple fact of slaves found on board."[6] Slave captains could avoid arrest or payment of hefty penalties by ordering a mass drowning of every slave on board. To prevent these deadly actions, the British entered into a very effective treaty with Spain in

1835. The "Equipment Clause" allowed naval officers to seize vessels that had equipment typical for slave ships. The type of equipment included spare planks fitted for a slave deck; more water casks and mess tubs than the crew would need; shackles, boats, handcuffs; and a large quantity of rice or other foods.

The U.S. Navy deployed a West African squadron, which had limited success initially. But in the 1830s, the Navy added to its antislavery squadron, including faster steamships. Van Buren sent cruisers to the African coast to detect any slave ships that falsely hoisted the American flag.[7] Despite these efforts, the slave trade escalated from 100,000 slaves per year, when it was legal, to 200,000 a year in 1839, when it was not.[8] Approximately 150,000 of those slaves crossed the Atlantic.[9]

Abolitionism in the *Amistad* Era

Some American abolitionists advocated "colonization," or providing transportation to freed blacks who wanted to return to Africa. The movement's premise was that blacks could not live in America without facing prejudice. Between 1822 and the Civil War, an estimated 15,000 African Americans settled in Liberia, a safe region on the west coast of Africa.

Not all African Americans welcomed colonization, viewing it as "deportation."[10] By the 1820s, most American slaves had been born in the United States; many had ancestry in America that dated back more than a century.[11] The Reverend Richard Allen, the first bishop of the African Methodist Episcopal church, explained the perspective of opponents of colonization: "This land which we have watered with our tears and our blood is now our mother country, and we are well satisfied to stay."[12] Many abolitionists who initially supported colonization ultimately rejected it in favor of emancipation.

During the 1820s and 1830s, due to a moral and religious revival, a growing number of abolitionists abandoned the goal of gradual emancipation. Instead, they prefered immediate abolition. This was known as the immediatist movement. In the 1830s, William Lloyd Garrison, a famous abolitionist and Baptist, started publishing *The Liberator*, a Boston newspaper that promoted immediatism.

Garrison, along with others, including wealthy, evangelical-minded Arthur Tappan, established the American Antislavery Society (AAS), a national organization. Hundreds of local abolition groups sprang up, as did more antislavery publications. At its peak, the abolition movement had perhaps 200,000 members.

Abolitionists faced much resistance. Throughout the 1830s, pro-slavery forces suppressed antislavery activities, often with violent acts. Mobs stormed into abolitionist meetings. Death threats were made against Garrison, Arthur Tappan, and his brother Lewis, also a wealthy evangelical. Vandals ransacked Lewis Tappan's home. A crowd destroyed three printing presses belonging to Elijah Lovejoy, an abolitionist newspaper editor in Alton, Illinois. They shot and killed Lovejoy when he tried to defend his fourth press.

Southern mobs seized and burned abolitionist mail from local post offices. The U.S. postmaster general permitted local Southern authorities to remove antislavery literature from the U.S. mails. President Andrew Jackson

William Lloyd Garrison, a noted abolitionist, promoted the immediate ending of slavery in his newspaper, *The Liberator.*

Slave Revolts

Following the successful Haitian Revolution by slaves and their freed relatives between 1791 and 1804, Southerners widely believed that antislavery messages would provoke slaves to revolt. They especially feared literate slaves, who might read or produce abolitionist materials. One example was David Walker. Born free in North Carolina, Walker circulated his *Appeal to the Coloured Citizens of the World*, in 1829. It outlined methods for conducting a revolt.

Of the nearly five hundred documented slave rebellions, three well-known instances involved literate blacks. Gabriel (whose owner's last name was Prosser) in 1800, and Denmark Vesey, a free man in 1822, planned revolts in the South. In both instances, other slaves revealed the plots, and the leaders were executed. Nat Turner was a literate slave who, along with six others, traveled to a number of Virginia plantations in 1831. They freed slaves and killed about sixty white people over a two-day period. Turner at first eluded capture, but was later found and executed.

Each attempted revolt sent shivers throughout the South. Nat Turner's rebellion prompted antiliteracy laws geared at making it extremely difficult for free blacks and slaves to learn to read.

sought a law that would prohibit the circulation through the mails in Southern states of "incendiary publications intended to instigate the slaves to insurrection."[13] Although the law did not pass, the climate of censorship angered Northerners.

Censorship extended to the halls of Congress. Between 1836 and 1844, the pro-slavery forces in Congress enforced a "gag rule" against receiving antislavery petitions. The gag rule existed in various forms, all intended to silence discussions about slavery and any action toward abolishing it.

Congressman James Henry Hammond of South Carolina argued that slavery could not be abolished in the United States. Hammond noted that freed slaves would have to be given compensation, which would be impossibly expensive. In addition, slavery was the foundation of the Southern economy. The idea of abolition was frightening, because it would set free "millions of systematically mistreated people."[14] Unlike in England and France, the freed slaves were not on distant islands, but they comprised about one-sixth of the American population.[15] Racism posed another obstacle to achieving emancipation.

Besides opposition from pro-slavery forces, the abolitionist movement had friction within its own ranks. Opinions differed regarding whether abolition should be gradual or immediate. While some abolitionists welcomed women, others did not. And some considered Garrison's views—such as calling the Constitution a "document of slavery"—to be radical.[16] As a result of these disagreements, the Tappan brothers left the AAS to form new antislavery societies. Thus, at the time

Lewis Tappan, who helped found the American Anti-Slavery Society, was instrumental in pursuing the rights of the Africans in the *Amistad* case.

the *Amistad* Africans arrived in the United States, the abolition movement was fractured. It needed something to bring it together.

Forming the *Amistad* Committee

When Judson held the hearing on the USS *Washington*, Dwight Janes, an abolitionist from New London, was present, probably as a customs officer.[17] Ruiz privately admitted to Janes that Antonio was the only black onboard who could speak Spanish. Both Ruiz and Antonio admitted that the blacks were recently from Africa. Janes understood what this meant: the blacks had been brought to Cuba illegally, in violation of the treaty outlawing the importation of slaves into Cuba.

Janes wrote to Joshua Leavitt of New York, a Yale graduate, lawyer, Congregationalist minister, and editor of the *Emancipator*, an abolitionist newspaper. He also sent a letter to Roger Sherman Baldwin, an antislavery New Haven attorney. Janes wanted Baldwin to take the case, and he asked Leavitt to find an interpreter so that the Africans could tell their story.

In his correspondence, Janes outlined legal arguments, all aimed at freeing the Africans and returning them home. Sending the *Amistad* blacks back to Africa was distinguishable from colonization, which evangelical abolitionists opposed. The abolitionist position was that *Amistad* captives had never been slaves or residents in America, and they were entitled to freedom in their homeland, where they had tried to go after the mutiny.[18]

One week after the hearing, the *Amistad* Committee was formed to finance the Africans' defense, education, and needs while in custody. Along with Joshua Leavitt, Lewis Tappan and Simeon Jocelyn headed the committee. Tappan was a wealthy New York businessman and leading abolitionist. Jocelyn was a Congregational minister, founder of New Haven's antislavery society, and a conductor on the Underground Railroad, which helped fugitive slaves escape to freedom. The committee planned to use the case as a means to garner support for immediate emancipation.[19]

The committee quickly published "Appeal to the Friends of Liberty," requesting donations for the Africans. Baldwin agreed to take the case, assisted by attorneys Seth P. Staples and Theodore Sedgwick. Tappan located John Ferry, a native African in New York, and brought him to see the *Amistad* Africans in the New Haven jail. Ferry was able to communicate well enough with them to learn that the children were African-born and kidnapped from there into Cuban slavery. But the Africans needed a better interpreter if they were ever going to be able to tell their stories in court.

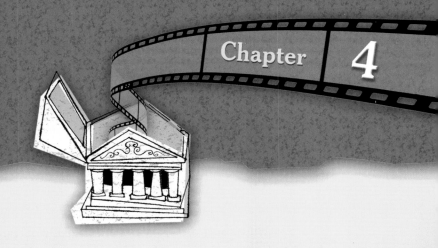

Chapter 4

The Legal Fight for Freedom

To the abolitionists' delight, the *Amistad* case stirred much excitement in the otherwise quiet town of Hartford, Connecticut. Some newspapers portrayed Ruiz and Montes as victims.[1] Other articles aroused sympathy for the Africans and called Cinque a hero.[2] Within ten days of the Africans' arrival, a new play entitled *The Black Schooner, or the Pirate Slaver Amistad* opened in New York, packing theaters throughout the fall.

Amid the media frenzy, people clamored for a glimpse of the Africans. More than four thousand visitors paid an admission of twelve cents to see them. Artists created large pictures representing the mutiny.

Nathaniel Jocelyn, the younger brother of Simeon from the *Amistad* Committee, painted a portrait of Cinque. Vendors sold engravings of the artworks as souvenirs for the crowds who filled the streets and hotels.

The Africans allowed a wax museum to take casts of their faces. The wax figures traveled the country. The casts were examined by a phrenologist, a person who assessed personality traits based on the shape of the skull. (In that era, phrenology was an accepted science.)

In the meantime, the *Amistad* Committee employed the Reverend George Day, former professor at the New York Institution for the Deaf and Dumb, to oversee the captives' religious and intellectual instruction. He communicated with the Africans through sign language. Yale Divinity students taught English, Bible studies, and other subjects, to the Africans, who lived in the New Haven jail. Several had died in custody, suffering from lingering symptoms of their time on the *Amistad*.[3]

Every day, the jailers brought the surviving Africans outside to the town's green for exercise. Onlookers watched as they leapt and somersaulted. Cinque performed "astonishing feats of agility."[4]

Legal Claims

Although the Africans began to act freer, their legal hurdles to freedom grew. Calderón, the Spanish minister, wanted the blacks to be sent to Havana for trial under Spanish law rather than having a U.S. trial. He relied on Pinckney's Treaty of 1795, a commercial pact between Spain and the United States. This treaty required nations to restore "all ships and merchandise"

Africans from the *Amistad* amuse the citizens of New Haven with wrestling and tumbling. The case stirred a great deal of excitement in the Connecticut town.

rescued from pirates or robbers on the high seas to the owners.

Secretary of State John Forsyth, a slavery supporter and former minister to Spain, conferred with other government officials. They recommended that Van Buren comply with Spain's demands based on Pinckney's Treaty. Van Buren was neutral toward slavery, but he did not want to alienate Southern voters.

Felix Grundy, the attorney general, summed up the administration's stance: Spain's demands were just, the U.S. government could not question the authenticity of the papers on a Spanish ship, and the blacks should be delivered to the Spanish minister.[5]

In line with the official position, Holabird, the district attorney and a slavery proponent, asked the court to order the restoration of the *Amistad* and its cargo, including the Africans, to Spain. Holabird further requested, in the alternative, that if it appeared the blacks had been brought from Africa in violation of the laws of the United States, then the court should order their return to Africa. The administration wanted the Africans out of the country; whether they were sent to Spain or Africa did not matter.

Spain's viewpoint, and the United States' receptiveness to it, troubled the Africans' supporters. They feared that Van Buren and Forsyth might issue an executive order handing the Africans to Spain "as fugitives from justice."[6] The defense attorneys sent a letter to the president, protesting any cooperation with the Spanish minister's demand. For its own political reasons, the United States was unwilling to consider the defense's position.

Alternate Arguments

Holabird made two distinct requests on behalf of the government: that the court should send the blacks either to Spain or to Africa, depending on the court's findings. Attorneys often make these types of alternate arguments when more than one result would be acceptable to their clients. It is not improper for a lawyer to make different, even conflicting arguments. In fact, attorneys are bound by professional ethics codes to be zealous advocates. This means that attorneys must make the best available and legitimate arguments for the people they represent.

Spain would not back down. Engaged in its own civil war, Spain needed to appear strong in international affairs.[7] A quick resolution would keep attention away from Spain's violation of an Anglo-Spanish treaty. By payment of two million dollars, Britain had induced Spain to cease slave trading. Spain knew that the *Amistad* case would raise Britain's ire, particularly against Cuba.[8]

Many other issues arose. Ruiz and Montes filed claims to the Africans as their slaves. They too relied on Pinckney's Treaty. They said that they had legally purchased the blacks in Havana. Gedney and his crew sought salvage, as did Green and the seamen who met the Africans on Long Island.

Captain Ferrer's family made a claim for Antonio. Cuban and Spanish merchants wanted their property that was aboard the *Amistad*. The blacks, except Antonio, responded by denying that they were slaves, or property of Ruiz and Montes. They also disputed the court's right to exercise jurisdiction over them.

On the first day of court, throngs of people lined up along the banks of the Connecticut River to greet the trial participants. Ruiz, Montes, and Gedney arrived by paddle steamboat and the Africans by canal boat.

The Africans had an inkling of what to expect in court because they were familiar with legal proceedings. By the early nineteenth century, Mende society had a well-established legal system, complete with public trials and enumerated rights like those contained in the Bill of Rights.[9] But with so many claimants and attorneys involved in the *Amistad* case, the circuit court took on a "circus-like atmosphere."[10]

Murder, Piracy, and the Great Writ

The case began before two federal judges. Courts only preside over the types of cases in which they specialize. Among other litigation, district courts in *Amistad* times handled admiralty cases. The U.S. district court, led by Judson, would decide the property and salvage issues at trial.

Circuit courts heard most cases involving federal crimes and some appeals from district courts. The U.S. circuit court, led by Smith Thompson, who was also on the U.S. Supreme Court, would advise the grand jury regarding legal questions about the murder and piracy charges.

A Poem in the *Emancipator*

To coincide with the first day in court, September 19, 1839, the *Emancipator* printed a poem by William Cullen Bryant, abolitionist and famous poet. It was revised from a ballad entitled "The African Chief."

Chained in a foreign land he stood,
A man of giant frame,
Amid the gathering multitude
That shrunk to hear his name—
All stern of look and strong of limb,
His dark eye on the ground—
And silently they gazed on him
As on a lion bound.

Vainly, but well, that chief had fought—
He was a captive now;
Yet pride, that fortune humbles not,
Was written on his brow.
The scars his dark broad bosom wore
Showed warrior true and brave;
A prince among his tribe before,
He could not be a slave.

The Africans' attorneys asked Thompson for a writ of *habeas corpus* directing the release of Teme, Kagne, and Margru, three young girls. Known as the "Great Writ," *habeas corpus* (Latin for "you should have the body") is a legal device for challenging unlawful imprisonment by the federal government. Baldwin told the court that the girls, who took no part in the mutiny, were being held unlawfully as property.[11]

Early in his career, Baldwin had succeeded in a *habeas corpus* action for an alleged runaway slave.[12] However, this *habeas corpus* had little chance of success. Thompson could deny it if he found any legal basis for holding the girls in custody.

At a minimum, the application would garner public sympathy. It would draw attention to the fact that the girls, probably all under eleven years old, were too young to have been residents of Cuba before the 1820 ban on slave trading. The girls could not speak Spanish, making it unlikely that they were legal slaves born in Cuba. They sat weeping, and evidently afraid, in the crowded courtroom. Their New Haven jailer, Colonel Pendleton, offered them fruit to calm them down.

The defense attorneys deliberately made lengthy arguments for several days. Although they hoped to win, they also wanted the newspaper coverage. While the attorneys argued about the *habeas corpus* petition, in another room the grand jury weighed the testimony of Ruiz, Montes, and Antonio. The grand jury decided that the blacks had killed the captain and the cook and stolen goods aboard the *Amistad* for their own use. But later the same afternoon, the judge announced that he was not going to enter formal criminal charges. Thompson held, as Baldwin had argued, that Spain's courts had to preside over any violation of its laws on a Spanish vessel. He said that a court in the United States had no power to decide a case involving possible mutiny and murder in international waters when no American citizens were involved. Thompson then dismissed the grand jury.

Thompson's decision terminated the criminal case within the United States. However, the property claims and the *habeas corpus* petition—which now included all the Africans—remained.

After expressing his personal hatred for slavery, Thompson announced that the law compelled him to retain custody of the Africans. The grand jury had found that Gedney seized the *Amistad* one mile from shore, which is considered the "high seas." Under these circumstances, admiralty jurisdiction enabled any district court to preside over the property claims to the schooner, its cargo, and the Africans.

In denying the *habeas corpus* petition, Thompson intended the question of the Africans' freedom to remain in litigation. This would enable the Supreme Court to make the ultimate determination, if necessary. Before reaching his decision, Thompson had voiced concern for the Africans' well-being if released. Keeping the Africans in custody obligated the court to provide necessities to them.[13]

Judson would have let the prisoners out on bail because they no longer faced criminal charges. He would have based the amount of bail on each African's estimated value as a slave in the Cuban market. The defense attorneys refused to consent. They believed this type of bail was equivalent to placing a monetary value

The Prudence Crandall Case

Abolitionists worried about Judson's involvement in the *Amistad* case. They believed that Judson was racially prejudiced based on arguments he had made in the Prudence Crandall matter a few years earlier. Crandall was a teacher who had operated a school for black girls in Canterbury, Connecticut.

People threw rotten eggs and stones at her windows, stage drivers refused to take students to her school, and local businesses would not sell items to her.[14] At the prompting of residents who feared an increase in the town's black population, the legislature in 1833 passed the "Connecticut Black Law." This made it a punishable offense for any person to establish a school for black people from other states and countries.

Crandall was arrested under the Black Law. Judson argued at the trial that Crandall's school would promote the integration of the races and encourage slave rebellions in the South.[15] Although a jury convicted Crandall, a court later reversed her conviction because the charges failed to make all the legally required allegations.

When the case ended, her opponents vandalized and attempted to burn Crandall's home. She finally gave up her school and left town. The episode altered opinions in that region. It became the strongest antislavery part of Connecticut.[16] The legislature struck down the Connecticut Black Law in 1838. The Crandall case illustrated that nearly fifty years after the Constitution guaranteed "equal rights," the application of the concept still depended on skin color.

on the Africans. The males stayed in New Haven jail. The three girls moved into the home of Pendleton and his wife.

Judson scheduled the next date in district court for November. He also ordered counsel to go to Montauk Point and investigate where the seizure of the *Amistad* was actually made.

Finding Interpreters

The *Amistad* Committee had an important task: to find interpreters who could communicate with the Africans better than John Ferry could. Dr. Josiah Gibbs, a Hebrew and linguistics professor at Yale College, visited the Africans in jail. He placed pennies in front of them until he was able to learn how to pronounce numbers in Mende and other dialects.[17]

Gibbs walked up and down the waterfronts of New Haven and New York for days, trying to find an African sailor. By late September, Gibbs came across James Covey and Charles Pratt, two Africans who worked on the *Buzzard*, a British warship docked in New York. Both could speak Mende and English.

Covey and Pratt spoke to the captives in jail. The Africans joyously responded to hearing their own language.[18] The interpreters prepared a brief write-up of each African's life. It was now possible for them to tell their stories in court.

More Legal Maneuvers

For ongoing publicity, defense counsel brought lawsuits against Ruiz and Montes on behalf of two of the Africans. They sought money from the Spaniards for false

Roger Sherman Baldwin, an antislavery attorney, defended the Africans in the *Amistad* case.

imprisonment, assault, and battery. On October 17, Tappan accompanied the sheriff's deputy during the arrest of Ruiz and Montes at a New York City hotel. The Spaniards did not pay the bail of $1,000 apiece, so they went to jail.

The arrests infuriated the new Spanish minister, Pedro Argaiz, who sent an angry letter to Forsyth. The pro-slavery press printed scathing articles, stating that this legal maneuver was "a ruse."[19] They called for putting Lewis Tappan in a "lunatic asylum."[20]

Judge Inglis of the New York court of common pleas decided to allow trials of Ruiz and Montes. He released Montes on low bail, and set Ruiz's bail at $250. Montes immediately fled back to Cuba. Ruiz refused to pay, hoping that he would gain sympathy if he remained in jail. Four months later, he posted bail and returned to Cuba. The trials never happened.

Back in district court, Baldwin tried to get the case dismissed. Gedney had seized the blacks in New York, a free state, and then unlawfully brought them to Connecticut, he said. Baldwin also pushed, in the alternative, for the trial to be in New York.

After hearing testimony on November 19 about where the *Washington* took over the *Amistad*, Judson ruled that the ship had been seized on the high seas, not New York waters. He held that the case could be tried in any district court in Connecticut. Judson then changed the trial location to New Haven. He postponed the case to January 7 due to the illness of Covey, the interpreter.

Aware of the *Amistad* proceedings, in January the British government sent a letter to the Spanish government in Madrid. The purpose was to convey the queen of England's expectation that the queen of Spain would enforce the law against Ruiz and Montes and any Spanish subjects who took part in the illegal slave trade.[21]

Recently Imported Africans

When the trial resumed in January, spectators flocked to the courthouse. The defense focused on proving that the blacks had been illegally imported from Africa. Dr. Richard R. Madden, the head of the British Antislavery Commission in Havana, was a key witness.

Because the January trial conflicted with Madden's schedule, Judson took his testimony in November at a deposition. A witness at a deposition is questioned under oath, before a trial occurs. At Madden's deposition, attorneys for all interested parties were present. Holabird was allowed to cross-examine Madden. Baldwin introduced the written transcript of Madden's deposition testimony during the trial.

For more than three years, the Irish-born Madden had lived in Havana. There, he was the superintendent of liberated Africans, a position that made him well-acquainted with recently imported Africans. He had observed the *Amistad* Africans in custody. Madden had "no doubt" that they were *bozales*, Africans who were recently brought to Cuba.[22] They were legally free, having been imported after the ban in 1820.

Madden examined the *traspassos* obtained by Ruiz and Montes, authorizing them to transport fifty-three *ladinos* with designated Spanish names to Puerto Principe. Madden determined that these documents

Direct Examination and Cross-Examination

Direct examination is the initial questioning of a witness by the attorney who is presenting that witness. Cross-examination is the subsequent questioning of that same witness by the opposing attorney; it is an important tool for uncovering the truth. If a witness gives a consistent account of events on direct and cross-examination, it strengthens the witness's credibility. If a witness changes testimony on cross-examination, it can make the witness appear untruthful.

were fraudulent, because none of these Africans were *ladinos*. The term *ladinos* was completely inapplicable to the African children, too young to have been long-term residents of Cuba.

Madden described the barracoons, exclusively used for receiving and selling *bozales*. He had visited one of the barracoons in September. A person who worked at the slave mart confided to him that the *Amistad* blacks had been purchased there. Madden estimated that slave ships brought between twenty thousand and twenty-five thousand Africans into Cuba during his tenure on the antislavery commission.

During cross-examination, Madden testified that Africans did not continue to speak their native language for a long time on Cuban plantations. Instead, the Africans would quickly acquire Spanish. This testimony supported Madden's assertion that the *Amistad* Africans, who could not speak any Spanish, had been recently imported into Cuba.

On cross-examination, Madden explained how local authorities in Havana routinely accepted "ten dollars a head" per African, so that slave traders could transfer *bozales* to different destinations in Cuba. Madden said the fee is deemed a "voluntary contribution." Cuban officials could not require this payment, because of the law against slave importation. Madden's account established that the Spanish government was cooperating with slave dealers.

The defense called Dwight Janes, the abolitionist who had been present on the *Washington* during Judson's inquiry. Janes had followed Ruiz into the ship's cabin and asked if any of the blacks could speak Spanish. Ruiz replied, "No, they were just from Africa."[23] Sullivan Haley, who was also on the *Washington* (possibly as a customs officer like Janes), testified to overhearing the conversation between Ruiz and Janes.[24] Their testimony showed that Ruiz and Montes had knowingly misrepresented newly imported Africans as *ladinos*. Although the Spaniards were back in Cuba and no longer involved in the case, the defense still attacked their claims of legitimate ownership of the blacks.

The interpreters provided further evidence that the Africans were *bozales*. Both Covey and Pratt had spoken with the *Amistad* blacks. They had no doubts that they had recently come from Africa.

Professor Josiah Gibbs of the Yale College linguistics department took the witness stand. With Covey's assistance, Gibbs had developed a Mende vocabulary and had conversed with many of the Africans. Gibbs testified that they could not speak Spanish. From their "language and manners," Gibbs determined that they were native Africans, recently from Africa.[25]

Judson surprised the courtroom by stating that he was "fully convinced that the men were recently from Africa," and no further testimony was required on that fact.[26] It was Judson's second favorable ruling to the defense. In September, Judson had decided that there could be no claim of salvage for the Africans, because the court "had no power to sell these persons."[27]

Despite these rulings in favor of the defense, the secretary of state and the president were convinced that Judson would grant Spain's demands. They had made secret travel arrangements to send the blacks to Cuba in the USS *Grampus*. Van Buren ordered the ship to wait in New London harbor. Forsyth instructed the U.S. marshal to deliver the Africans to the *Grampus* immediately after the verdict. The plan was to whisk the

Expert Witness

In legal terms, Professor Gibbs was an "expert witness." This means that he had specialized knowledge, based on his training, education, or experience, that enabled him to speak with authority about a certain subject. An expert witness's testimony is offered to explain matters that are not within the everyday knowledge of most citizens.

Africans away before the defense had time to file an appeal.

The commander of the *Grampus* warned them that it was too small to accommodate all the prisoners below in the hold. He said that anyone on the decks would be swept overboard. The Van Buren administration disregarded the commander's concerns.

Long-Awaited Testimony

By the time he testified, Cinque had achieved folk-hero status. The press depicted him as having absolute authority over the other Africans, "but exercised with justice and mildness."[28] People called him the Black Prince. Cinque attracted such curiosity that artist Nathaniel Jocelyn took out an advertisement requesting no interruptions when he painted the mutiny leader's portrait.[29]

From the moment he stood, Cinque riveted the courtroom. With Covey as the interpreter, Cinque told how he had been kidnapped near his home, sold, and brought to Lomboko.[30] He described his voyage on the *Tecora*.

At times during Cinque's testimony, Covey did not have to provide translation. Cinque's gestures conveyed more than words. He hunched his body and pulled his hands and feet together to demonstrate what it was like to be manacled for long periods of time in packed quarters on a slave ship. Cinque showed with his hands the degrading manual inspection that Ruiz conducted in Havana to assess whether the Africans were healthy. He spoke about the mistreatment on the *Amistad*, the mutiny, and the capture by Gedney.

A mural of the *Amistad* trial by painter Hale Woodruff,
which hangs in Talledega College in Alabama.

Slaves being inspected prior to sale. During the trial, Cinque was able to convey the degradation of this process without using words.

"Give us free! Give us free!"[31] Cinque declared at one point in the proceedings.

Two other Africans, Fuliwa and Grabeau, testified to the same facts as Cinque.[32] Grabeau, who was second in command, described the scene on Long Island, when the Africans tried to get Green to take them back to Sierra Leone. Fuliwa told how Celestino, the cook, had said that the blacks would be killed and eaten.

The District Attorney's Evidence

District Attorney William Holabird presented evidence, but much of it wound up boosting the defense. Antonio, Captain Ferrer's slave, testified about the mutiny. His account did not help the prosecution. He acknowledged that the cook, communicating with signs, had told the blacks that they would be killed and eaten. He said that the *Amistad* carried slaves every two months. Antonio contradicted earlier statements he had made about who killed the captain.[33]

"Give us free! Give us free!" Cinque declared at one point in the proceedings.

The deposition of Antonio Vega, the Spanish consul, harmed the prosecution's case. Vega had resided in Cuba for several years. He claimed that in Cuba there was no law "considered in force" that prohibited anyone from importing African slaves.[34] He said that newly imported Africans were "constantly brought" to Cuba, and were legally transferred once there.

Contrary to Madden's deposition, Vega claimed that slaves continued speaking in their native language on plantations for years. Vega also vouched for the papers of the *Amistad*, which he said were in the "usual form." Vega said that it was not necessary to practice any fraud to obtain these papers.

To rebut Vega's account, Dwight Janes testified for the defense about a conversation with Vega. Janes had asked Vega in New London when the slave trade was prohibited. Vega believed it was in 1814, but did not know the penalty.[35] This was an admission from Vega that he knew it was illegal to import African slaves into Cuba. Vega's testimony aided the defense, rather than the prosecution, because it showed that the Cubans were widely ignoring an existing treaty.

U.S. Marshal Norris Willcox testified about the value of the *Amistad* and its cargo, excluding the Africans. In depositions, the seamen aboard the *Washington* gave detailed accounts of the seizure of the Africans off Long Island.

Closing Arguments

After five days of testimony and evidence, the attorneys made their final arguments. Gedney and Meade's counsel, W. F. Brainard, argued that regardless of whether Ruiz and Montes lawfully owned the blacks, the United States should deliver them to Spain. He reasoned that Spain's laws govern criminal violations on a Spanish vessel. Gedney and Meade had performed "meritorious services," according to their attorneys, entitling them to salvage.[36]

The attorneys were aware of the overwhelming sympathy for the Africans, as well as the media reports and criticism of their clients for seeking salvage on humans. General Isham, also representing Gedney and Meade, stated that his clients would "never receive salvage on human flesh," but that they should be granted reasonable compensation, nonetheless, for preserving the Spaniards' property.[37]

Green's lawyer, Governor William W. Ellsworth, claimed that his client's sentiments were against the delivery of the Africans to Spain or the United States government. He argued, however, that if such delivery occurred, Green's entitlement to salvage took priority over other claims. Green, he said, had performed a more "valuable and hazardous service" than Gedney and the others.[38]

William P. Cleveland, representing Cuban merchants who had shipped cargo on the *Amistad*, opposed Gedney and Meade's right to salvage. He said that the *Washington* was serving the United States, and was obligated to provide assistance without compensation.[39] Green should not receive any reward, he said, because he had only attempted to save the *Amistad*, but had not succeeded in doing so.

Holabird argued on behalf of the Spanish minister that Pinckney's Treaty required the United States to surrender the Africans to Spain. He said that the *Amistad*'s papers proved the Africans were slaves and stated that Spanish law did not forbid slavery.[40]

All three defense attorneys made closing arguments. They said that the Africans were born free and were entitled to their freedom. The licenses to transport them were not authentic, and were based on the misrepresentation of the blacks as *ladinos*. When the Africans were seized on Long Island, they were not slaves, and could not be called slaves now. The Spanish minister was wrongfully interfering in the case.

The evidence was in. The arguments had been made. Throughout the months, the Africans expressed anxiety over their uncertain future and the thought of returning to Havana.[41] Their fate was up to Judge Judson.

Chapter 5

The Final Legal Battle

After taking the weekend to mull over the case, Judson read his decision on Monday, January 13, 1840. Like the circuit court, Judson held that the district court had jurisdiction over the admiralty claims because Gedney had seized the *Amistad* on the high seas.

In the rest of the multi-part decision, Judson:

- Rejected the claims of Green and the other seamen to salvage.
- Dismissed the claims of Gedney and the crew of the *Washington* for salvage on the Africans.

- Granted the salvage claim of Gedney and the *Washington*'s crew, at a rate of one-third of the gross proceeds of the *Amistad* and the cargo, which would have been lost if the ship had remained at sea.
- Granted the claims of Cuban merchants for return of specified cargo of the *Amistad*.
- Denied all claims of Ruiz, Montes, and the United States that were made on Spain's behalf.
- Denied the claim of the Spanish minister demanding the surrender of the Africans.
- Granted the claim of the vice consul of Spain, requesting Antonio's surrender to Spain.

Judson found that the Africans were not slaves, but were free-born natives of Africa. He held that the Africans were never residents of Cuba or subjects of Spain. They were kidnapped from their homes, in violation of their rights and the laws of Spain. Ruiz and Montes unlawfully transported them, using inaccurate passports. They revolted on the *Amistad* to regain their liberty. Judson said, "Cinquez and Grabeau shall not sigh for Africa in vain. Bloody as may be their hands, they shall yet embrace their kindred."[1]

Judson put the Africans in the custody of the U.S. marshal, to be delivered to the president for transport to Africa. The abolitionists would have preferred if the judge had granted the Africans' freedom without specifying that the president had to return them to Africa.[2] Further upsetting the abolitionists, Judson had determined that Antonio was legally a slave, to be returned as property under Pinckney's Treaty.[3]

The Africans were in the jail when the judge gave his verdict. A member of the *Amistad* Committee rushed to tell them that the court had declared them free and ordered them to be sent back to Africa. On hearing the judge's decision, they threw themselves at the feet of the person who brought the good news.

The verdict shocked and upset President Van Buren. Secretary of State Forsyth quickly ordered an appeal from the decision, except for the part pertaining to Antonio. Because of the administration's filing of this appeal, the Africans' joy about Judson's decision soon turned into disappointment. Even worse for the Africans, the United States had long dropped its initial request that the Africans be sent either to Spain or Africa. Now, the administration only wanted the Africans in Spain's custody, which likely would have meant a return to slavery or possibly execution.

In April 1840, the appeal went before Judge Thompson of the circuit court. The Africans' attorneys alleged that the United States had no right to make claims on behalf of Spanish citizens. Thompson affirmed Judson's opinion. Thompson thought that the Supreme Court should decide the case.

The Africans would have to wait many months for an outcome. The Supreme Court's next session was not until January 1841. In the interim, they enthusiastically continued their studies. They loved to read books, and they complained if the lessons ended too early.

Preparing for Supreme Court Argument

The *Amistad* Committee wanted a nationally known lawyer to argue the case alongside Baldwin. They

President Martin Van Buren. The verdict shocked Van Buren, and his secretary of state filed an appeal for a new trial.

considered Daniel Webster and Rufus Choate. However, both were unsympathetic to abolitionist ideas and busy with other commitments.[4] Their third choice was John Quincy Adams, the former president (1825–1829). Adams believed that slavery was "the great and foul stain upon the North American Union."[5]

Adams had been following the story in the press. After the *habeas corpus* decision, Ellis Gray Loring, an abolitionist from Boston and the Tappans' attorney, consulted Adams about the case.[6] Adams wrote in his diary on October 1, 1839, that it "now absorbs a great part of my time, and all my good feelings."[7]

In October 1840, Tappan and Loring visited Adams at his Massachusetts home. They asked him to make the Africans' argument in the highest court. Known as "Old Man Eloquent," Adams was a seventy-four-year-old senator. Thirty years had passed since he last appeared before the Supreme Court.

Believing in the cause but not in his own ability to perform the job, Adams reluctantly accepted. His diary bemoans, "The life I lead is trying on my constitution.

Dramatic License

The movie makes it seem as if the *Amistad* Committee hounded John Quincy Adams to become involved in the case. In reality, they were happy to have him on their team, but he was not their first choice.

My eyes are threatening to fail me. My hands tremble like an aspen-leaf. My memory daily deserts me."[8] But he hoped that he would prove himself "in every respect equal to the task."[9]

Adams turned out to be a worthy choice. Not only had he been the president, he was the son of a former president. In his youth, he traveled through Europe, translating conversations between foreign ministers.[10] After practicing law in Boston, Adams held appointments in the Netherlands, the United Kingdom, Portugal, and Russia. His background uniquely equipped him to understand diplomacy and international relations.[11]

Adams also had a solid grasp of domestic politics. Early in his career, he was a state senator for the Massachusetts Federalists. After angering the party with his outspokenness, he was sent to the U.S. Senate. He held one term as president of the United States. Later, he was elected to Congress, where he served for seventeen years. Adams constantly infuriated pro-slavery forces in Congress. He received death threats over his unrelenting opposition to the "gag rule."

The Trial of One President by Another

Once Adams became involved, the *Amistad* case was called the "trial of one president by another."[12] Van Buren wanted Judson's decision reversed because it had caused him embarrassment. However, by the time of the Supreme Court argument, Van Buren was an outgoing president, a "lame duck."

Van Buren's bid for reelection in 1840 faced obstacles. Not long into his presidency, the country experienced a financial depression, known as the Panic of 1837.

The nation was split over many issues, such as western expansion and slavery, including the *Amistad* episode.

Van Buren could not counteract the successful campaign of William Henry Harrison, the Whigs' nominee. Harrison was a national hero who had defended settlements against Indians, most famously in the Battle of Tippecanoe.

The inclusion of a third-party candidate also harmed Van Buren. The abolitionists formed the Liberty Party in 1839, dedicated to eliminating slavery. Their nominee took some votes away from Van Buren. Despite the electoral defeat, Van Buren's administration continued its stance regarding the *Amistad* Africans.

The Supreme Court

As the highest court in the United States, the Supreme Court does not reconsider the facts of the case. It is an appeals court that only hears appeals addressing constitutional issues. The Supreme Court interprets the U.S. Constitution. It enforces the rights and protections guaranteed in the Declaration of Independence and the Constitution. Examples include freedom of speech, freedom of religion, the right to privacy, and the right to equality. The *Amistad* case fell under Supreme Court jurisdiction because it involved freedom and basic rights.

Unlike in trial courts, the attorneys do not present witnesses or evidence to the Supreme Court. Instead, they submit written briefs, containing arguments based on the testimony, evidence, and verdicts from the lower courts.

Lawyers also make oral arguments to the Supreme Court. There are nine Supreme Court justices, whom

Former president John Quincy Adams, an antislavery advocate who argued the *Amistad* case before the Supreme Court.

the president appoints. In modern practice, the justices interrupt lawyers during their oral arguments to ask questions about the case.

Unlike the days of the lengthy *Amistad* arguments, today the Supreme Court imposes strict rules: only one attorney is allowed to argue for each side and arguments must be short.[13] Larger caseloads caused the Court to limit oral argument to two hours per side in 1849, one hour in 1925, and a half hour since 1970.

In advance of the argument date, parties nowadays may request additional time for "divided arguments," or two attorneys for one side, but such requests are rarely granted. After hearing arguments, the justices work together on reaching a decision. The decision does not have to be unanimous; it just needs the backing of a majority of the justices. Because the Supreme Court decides difficult issues, the decisions are sometimes split 5–4, with five justices in favor and four opposed. A justice may choose to write a dissenting opinion, if his or her viewpoint is in the minority. A justice may write a concurring opinion if he or she agrees with the majority, but uses different legal reasoning to reach the result.

Of the nine justices presiding over the *Amistad* case, five were from Southern states. The Chief Justice, Roger Taney, was an appointee of Andrew Jackson's who hailed from slave-owning tobacco farmers. Taney's legal opinions indicated that he viewed blacks as property rather than as persons entitled to equal rights with whites.[14]

New Yorker Smith Thompson, who presided over the circuit court proceedings, was a vocal opponent of slavery but a close friend of Van Buren. Joseph

Story of Massachusetts detested slavery but disliked abolitionists.[15] During the first half of the nineteenth century, Story was "the leading defender of civil liberties" on the Supreme Court.[16]

The Arguments

Henry Gilpin, who had recently replaced Felix Grundy as U.S. attorney general, opened the arguments. The ship's papers proved that the blacks were the property of Ruiz and Montes, he said. If there was any fraud in obtaining or issuing the passports, Spain should handle that matter. Gilpin argued that the United States should fulfill its treaty obligations by returning the blacks to Spain.

Baldwin told the court that the Africans were not property but were people who had freed themselves from unlawful bondage. Because freedom is a natural right, the laws of nature should govern the court's decision, Baldwin said. Baldwin repeated earlier arguments that the Africans were kidnapped and transported under fraudulent permits.

It was Adams's turn to speak. He had been preparing for this moment from the day he agreed to represent the Africans. He had reviewed legal documents and newspaper clippings. He had conferred with Baldwin and he had visited the Africans in Connecticut. After the visit, Kale (pronounced Ka-le), a boy who was one of the four children on the *Amistad*, sent Adams a letter. In it, he wrote, "All we want is make us free."[17]

Numerous delays gave Adams extra time to prepare. He needed every minute. On February 23, 1841, the day before his Supreme Court argument, Adams penned in his diary: "With increasing agitation of mind, now little short of agony, I rode . . . to the Capitol. . . . The very skeleton of my argument is not yet put together."[18] He later wrote that his anxiety continued until "the moment when I rose; and then my spirit did not sink within me."[19]

Early in his argument, Adams noted that Baldwin had argued so thoroughly "as leaves me scarcely anything to say."[20] Adams then spoke for more than eight hours over several days. Before Adams's second day of argument, Supreme Court Justice Philip Barbour died in his sleep. There was a break of a few days for the funeral.

Adams pointed at the Declaration of Independence, hanging in the courtroom. He said that it was the only law that should guide the court's determination.

Adams spent much time examining the letters between Forsyth and the Spanish ministers, Calderón and then Pedro Alcantara de Argaiz. Adams said the correspondence indicated the administration's sympathy for the slave traders. He claimed that the executive branch was interfering and was improperly complying with the demands of the Spanish minister. The presence of the *Grampus* indicated that the United States was willing to appease Spain at any cost. The *Grampus*'s own commander had warned that it was too small to hold all of the Africans safely.

Adams utilized several common legal techniques. First, he distinguished the *Amistad* facts from those of the *Antelope*, a case that Gilpin had cited. Slaves stolen from American and foreign slave ships had been found onboard the *Antelope*. The Supreme Court had held in the *Antelope* that international law permitted the slave trade; it decided that the American slaves should be freed but the others were property to be returned to their owners. After reviewing the facts of the *Antelope*, Adams argued that it had "peculiar circumstances," and it did not authorize the president to deliver the *Amistad* Africans to the Spanish minister.

Adams also interpreted the "legislative intent" of Pinckney's Treaty. Attorneys often analyze what the drafters of a law meant when they wrote the law. This analysis enables an attorney to argue that a certain case falls within the law, or that the legislation does not apply to the case. Adams focused on Article 9, the provision requiring nations to "restore entire" to the owner "all ships and merchandise . . . rescued" from "pirates or robbers on the high seas." Adams argued that Pinckney's Treaty was inapplicable because the word "merchandise" was not intended to include humans. He noted that the Africans could not, at the same time, be considered "merchandise" and "robbers." This would absurdly mean that they had stolen themselves, and they needed to be rescued from themselves. Furthermore, he said that the phrase "restore entire" made no sense as applied to people.

To prove that the term "merchandise" did not include people, Adams spoke from personal knowledge. Pinckney's Treaty was renewed in 1819 as the Adams-Onís Treaty. Adams participated in all of the negotiations with the minister of Spain. He said, "I am certain that neither of us ever entertained an idea that this word merchandise was to apply to human beings."[21]

In reply, Gilpin countered that the Adams-Onís Treaty contained the exact same provisions as the original enactment. Gilpin insisted that if any changes regarding "merchandise" had been contemplated, new clauses would have been added. Gilpin was clearly implying that, during the treaty negotiations, if Adams had meant to exclude human beings from the term "merchandise," then Adams should have specified or clarified the intentions of the law.

The Supreme Court's Decision

The Court reached its 7–1 decision in one week. On Friday, March 9, Justice Story read the opinion. It upheld the finding that Ruiz and Montes never lawfully owned the blacks. Their alleged purchase of the Africans was fraudulent. Pinckney's Treaty was inapplicable because the blacks were not pirates or robbers, but kidnap victims. The Court upheld the granting of salvage to Gedney.

Adams argued that Pinckney's Treaty was inapplicable because the word "merchandise" was not intended to include humans.

The circuit court had affirmed Judson's order for the president to send Cinque and the others to Africa. The Supreme Court reversed this order. The Court declared the Africans to be free and dismissed them from custody.

The decision did not discuss executive interference, which Adams had addressed at length. Nonetheless, Adams's argument made an impression on the judges. Story, writing to his wife, described Adams' argument as "extraordinary . . . for its power and bitter sarcasm, and its dealing with topics far beyond the record and points of discussion."[22]

After the decision, Adams wrote to Lewis Tappan. "The captives are free!" Crediting Tappan, he added, "Thanks! in the name of humanity and justice, to you." Adams never sent a bill for his services.[23]

The newspapers brought word of the decision before Adams's letter. When the Africans heard the news, they knelt in prayer.

Returning Home

The Africans were free, but they needed money to go home. Adams thought that the United States was morally obligated to pay for the Africans' trip. He also believed that the government should generously compensate the Africans for eighteen months of false imprisonment.[24] The new administration considered his suggestions but appeared unwilling to help without congressional approval.[25]

The *Amistad* Committee made new appeals for donations. People gave money, food, and clothes. The Africans had been living in Westville, Connecticut. In the spring of 1841, they moved to Farmington, Connecticut, an appropriate locale. It had two antislavery societies and hosted Underground Railroad activities.

The men lived in a barn converted into barracks. The girls lived with local families. They continued their studies and religious instruction. Some of the Africans traveled the country for a fundraising tour with committee members.

It was a bittersweet time for Lewis Tappan. The happiness of the verdict was balanced by grief. In May

The handwritten opinion of the Supreme Court in the case of *United States* v. *The Amistad*, ordering the immediate release of the captives.

1841, he went to the bedside of his eighteen-year-old daughter, who was dying of tuberculosis.[26] One week after she died, Tappan brought the Africans into the Broadway Tabernacle in New York. People paid fifty cents each to hear them spell, sing, read Bible verses, and give speeches.

The Africans grew more homesick. Foone, a good swimmer, drowned in a pond; he may have committed suicide. Others had noticed that he was depressed over the long separation from his family.

Most interactions with local residents were pleasant, but in at least one instance, some troublemakers instigated a fight with the Africans. Cinque had to restrain them.[27] In September, Tappan sensed that the Africans were ready to go home.[28]

Tappan sought members of the clergy to accompany the Africans home. The plan was to establish a Christian mission in Africa. Eventually five missionaries volunteered to go. By November, they raised $1,840 to charter a ship, the *Gentleman*, from New York.

At daybreak one November morning, the Africans boarded a steamboat that took them from Farmington to Staten Island. In a farewell ceremony held at the Broadway Tabernacle, Tappan read a letter from Adams, thanking the Africans for sending him a Bible in appreciation for his hard work.

On December 4, 1841, Tappan addressed the Africans aboard the *Gentleman* before they began their voyage. Cinque spoke on behalf of the Africans. People wept as they said goodbye to Tappan. After more than two years in America, the thirty-five surviving Africans, along with interpreter Covey, were headed home.

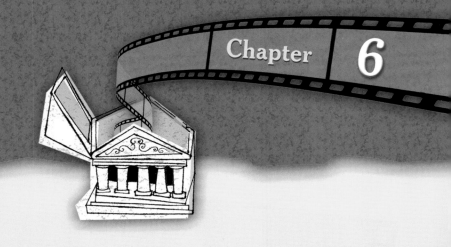

Chapter 6

Amistad: The Movie

The *Amistad* incident was not well-known, even to Sierra Leoneans, until the movie publicized it. Debbie Allen, the actress, choreographer, and producer, first came across a book about the mutiny in 1978. She obtained the movie rights to a fictionalized account, but Hollywood was unreceptive. Allen, an African American, took the rejection personally.

Allen brought the idea to director Steven Spielberg after his success with *Schindler's List*, a 1993 Academy Award winner about the Holocaust. Spielberg responded with enthusiasm. He said, "While making the film, I

In the movie *Amistad*, African actor Djimon Hounsou played Cinque.

never felt that I was telling someone else's story. I felt . . . that I was telling everyone's story—a story that people of all nationalities and races should know."[1]

The film has an all-star cast. It was shot primarily in Newport, Rhode Island, with a set designed to resemble New Haven in the 1830s. Scenes in Africa were filmed in Puerto Rico.

Djimon Hounsou (pronounced JIE-mon HAHN-soo) played Cinque. Hounsou was born in West Africa. At six feet, four inches, he is much taller than Cinque's five feet, eight inches. But critics acknowledged that Hounsou's commanding presence was comparable to Cinque's, and that he was well-cast.[2] Coincidentally, he portrayed the leader of another slave mutiny in *Ill-Gotten Gains*, an independent film also released in 1997.

Africans play the Mende men on the *Amistad*. Throughout the film, they are actually speaking in Mende. Samuel Pieh, who grew up in Sierra Leone, played one of the older Africans, Suuleh. Pieh claims to be the great-grandson of Sengbe Pieh (Cinque), even though some researchers cast doubt on this relationship.[3]

Real-life Supreme Court Justice Harry Blackmun portrayed Justice Joseph Story. At the time of filming, Blackmun was retired from the bench. He was on the Court from 1970 to 1994. Blackmun had the distinction of being the only Supreme Court Justice to have played one in a movie.

Reviews

The film opened to mixed reviews. Some praised the realism of the mutiny scene.[4] Others disliked the long courtroom scenes and Spielberg's handling of the legal developments.[5] Critics commended the aural and visual appeal, attributed to the musical score, cinematography, authentic sets, and costumes.[6] Reviews almost universally applauded Spielberg and Allen for making the film. Although some history books covered the subject, the movie made the story available to a wider audience.

Critic Roger Ebert felt that *Amistad* did not have the "emotional charge" of *Schindler's List.* He also thought it focused too much on the law and not enough on the victims. However, he credited *Amistad* for providing faces and names to the African characters, who are often "faceless victims" in movies.[7]

Hounsou received much acclaim for his performance. Yet one scholar noted that Hounsou infused his character with "seemingly endless rage," unlike the real Cinque.[8] Hounsou best conveys Cinque's true gentleness and strength in scenes that are completely fictional. Hounsou shows the calm demeanor of Cinque when he

Schooner Replica

The realism of the mutiny sequence was enhanced by the *Californian*, the 1840s-era replica sailing vessel used in the film. At 145 feet long and 101 feet high, the *Californian* is just 15 feet longer than the *Amistad.*[9] It was built in 1984 after the Nautical Heritage Society in Long Beach raised $1.5 million in donations.

visits Adams's home and in another scene in which he describes how he killed a lion.

Critic James Berardelli found the film compelling despite its lack of a "well-defined human villain."[10] Berardelli explained that although slavery was the enemy, "an ideology, no matter how evil, is rarely the best adversary."[11] Other critics wrote that the film had too many complex subplots.[12]

Amistad did not win an Academy Award, but it received four nominations: Sir Anthony Hopkins, as John Quincy Adams, for best supporting actor; Janusz Kaminski for best cinematography; Ruth E. Carter for best costume design; and John Williams for best original score.

Inaccuracies and Omissions

Dr. Clifton Johnson, founding director of the Amistad Research Center (now in New Orleans), was a historical consultant on the movie. He was "exasperated" by the film's historical inaccuracies in the guise of "dramatic license."[13] Some errors may be explained because the fictionalized book that Allen optioned for the movie, *Black Mutiny*, is not a scholarly source.[14] It does not contain footnotes, and the author admits to making up dialogue because the real conversations are unknown.

A movie is necessarily subject to time constraints. However, the film glossed over a fact that would only have increased the audience's sympathy for the Africans. It was not insignificant that Celestino cruelly joked with Cinque that the Africans would be cooked and eaten.[15] This gave Cinque an additional feeling of urgency to revolt, based on numerous tales throughout Africa that whites were cannibals.

Historians criticized the sporadic use of Mende subtitles during the film.[16] Oddly, translation is provided for the Spanish speakers but not for the Africans in the mutiny. The audience is thus able to understand the captors but not the victims, until a later scene when Mende subtitles appear.

A glaring inaccuracy was the creation of Theodore Joadson (Morgan Freeman), a former slave who became an abolitionist. Historians complained that there was no need to resort to fiction.[17] Black abolitionists existed, including the Reverend James W. C. Pennington, an educator and missionary. A former slave, Pennington became a pastor in New Haven. Pennington was involved in the *Amistad* case after the Supreme Court's decision. He organized support for African missions as the first president of the Union Missionary Society.

Another fabricated character was Judge Coglin (Jeremy Northam). Forsyth (David Paymer) and Van Buren (Nigel Hawthorne) bring Coglin in to replace Judson (Allan Rich). He was a "younger, more handsome, and presumably more obedient judge."[18] A president's act of replacing a judge in an individual case would have violated the separation of powers. To acknowledge this huge cinematic error, Joadson tells Adams, "I was under the mistaken impression that our judicial and executive branches were separate." Joadson may be a fictional character, but he knows a gross distortion of reality when he sees one.

Coglin, a devout Catholic, is a vehicle for some of the film's religious symbolism. Several scenes show him in

Director Steven Spielberg (on left) speaks with actors Anthony Hopkins, playing Adams, and Morgan Freeman, playing the fictional character of Theodore Joadson.

church, cleansing his hands and crossing himself at the altar.

In one scene, Cinque and Yamba (Razaaq Adoti) are reading an illustrated Bible in the jail. The audience might be wondering how they are able to read, because viewers are never informed that the Africans had received daily instructions in reading, writing, and religion from Yale Divinity School students. This scene transitions smoothly into the next shot of Coglin in church before he renders his decision. As the Africans head to court to hear Coglin's verdict, nuns cross themselves, and one of the Africans spies a ship mast that resembles a cross.

Some of the dialogue misrepresents the characters' true viewpoints. For example, when an adviser tries to inform Van Buren about the arrival of the *Amistad* Africans, the president dismisses the conversation. He says, "There are three to four million Negroes in this country. Why should I concern myself with these forty-four?" A founder of the Democratic Party, Van Buren was politically savvy. He understood what the case meant, and that it was receiving much attention in the newspapers. However, the film repeatedly misleads viewers to believe that the *Amistad* decision, if unfavorable to the South, would risk immediate civil war. The country was not quite ready for war at that point.

The movie focuses more on Adams's involvement in the case than on Tappan's. Tappan (Stellan Skarsgard) was the person most responsible for assembling the defense team and overseeing the care and education of the Africans while in the United States. He spearheaded the fundraising efforts for their return home, and made personal sacrifices in order to do so, none of which is conveyed. In one scene, Tappan implies to Joadson that the Africans might be better for the abolition movement as martyrs following execution. The real Tappan would never have made such a statement.

Although Queen Isabella II (Anna Paquin) was a child, the scenes in which she plays with dolls were invented. In one scene, the queen struggles to read aloud a letter bearing her signature but written by her advisers. The caricature was a means to convey that she was simply following her advisers' suggestions.

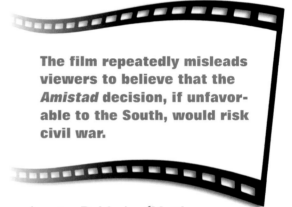

The film repeatedly misleads viewers to believe that the *Amistad* decision, if unfavorable to the South, would risk civil war.

Professor Gibbs (Austin Pendleton), the linguist, comes across as "bumbling" for comedic effect.[19] He tries to translate what the Africans are saying to Baldwin (Matthew McConaughey) by simply imitating their hand gestures. In another scene, Gibbs teaches Baldwin and Joadson how to count in Mende, and then they search the boardwalk for a Mende speaker. In reality, Gibbs, not Joadson or Baldwin, searched the ports for an interpreter.

Shortly after interpreter Covey (Chiwetel Ejiofor) meets Cinque, Baldwin asks Cinque about a story he heard from the others. The story is about how Cinque alone had killed a lion, the "most terrifying beast anyone has seen." Cinque tells the tale, for which there is no historical basis. He describes how he got lucky and threw a rock at the right spot on the lion. Cinque denies being brave against the lion. Baldwin disagrees, reminding Cinque about another instance of his bravery—the *Amistad* insurrection—which Baldwin calls the "other lion."

After receiving a signal from Baldwin, Joadson then hands Cinque a lion's tooth that he found earlier on the *Amistad*. We learn that Cinque's wife had given him this tooth. It sends Cinque into a flashback that reveals the events leading up to the mutiny. The flashback shows Cinque, admiring his wife and children, and then instantly being abducted and abused. Soon, he is at the Lomboko slave fortress, chained to many other Africans. While marching in chains, Cinque looks at the tooth around his waist, to remind the audience how we got into this flashback.

The *Tecora* scene includes events that did occur on slave ships. Although they may not have occurred on the *Tecora*, it is an understandable cinematic device. They illustrate the horrors of the Middle Passage. Effective camera work gives the viewers a sense of the jostling on the ships, and even a feeling of seasickness.

In the movie, before the case goes to the Supreme Court, Cinque visits Adams at his greenhouse. No interpreter is needed during this scene, thanks to the universal language of botany. In truth, Cinque never visited Adams's home or sniffed an African violet in his greenhouse. Furthermore, African violets—which have no scent—originated in East Africa.[20] As a West African native, Cinque would never have seen one before.[21]

After the verdict, the fictional character Captain Fitzgerald (Peter Firth) supervises the destruction of

Lomboko. In actuality, Commander Joseph Denman led the destruction in 1840, even before the *Amistad* case went to the Supreme Court. By inaccurately representing when the destruction occurred, the movie implies that there was a connection between the Supreme Court's decision and the burning of slave fortresses.

The film immediately shifts to the Africans aboard the *Gentleman*, headed home. Perhaps because of time limitations, the movie fails to explain how they managed to earn money to charter the ship, how long it took for them to do so, and what occupied their daily lives in the interim. The Supreme Court's decision was in March 1841, and the *Gentleman* did not arrive in Africa until January 1842. In between, they continued their studies and traveled around the country on fundraising tours. Theatergoers also do not learn of the plans to establish the Mende Mission or the positive results of all the mission activity in Sierra Leone.

Legal Flaws

The first courtroom scene involves different attorneys storming at seemingly random times, interrupting each other, and screaming out their claims. When Secretary of State Forsyth charges in, Judson seems in awe. But Forsyth never appeared in the Connecticut proceedings.

In reality, the first judicial involvement was the hearing on the USS *Washington*. The movie excludes the hearing, the *habeas corpus* action (except for occasional references to a "writ"), and the salvage claims of the Long Island sea captains. Though it makes the legal storyline simpler, in the process, it omits some details with emotional impact. For example, the *Amistad*

Matthew McConaughey, as defense attorney Roger Baldwin, with the *Amistad* captives.

children aroused much sympathy at the *habeas corpus* proceeding, a fact unknown to audiences. Likewise, the movie omits Antonio, Captain Ferrer's slave. Antonio had originally wanted to go back to slavery in Cuba. Indeed, Judson ordered this outcome. After Antonio's change of heart, Tappan helped him escape to freedom. This was another true fact that could have added tension to the plot.[22]

The film lumps the criminal charges in with the rest of the claims, to avoid having two judges and having to explain what happened with the grand jury. Forsyth says the "jury appears disposed to freeing them." This phrasing refers to a trial jury, which never existed. Once Thompson dismissed the grand jury and the criminal charges, it was a bench trial, meaning that the judge was deciding the case. The movie leaves viewers with the erroneous impression that the criminal case in the United States continued.

McConaughey was miscast as Baldwin. Unlike the twenty-eight-year-old actor, the real Baldwin was forty-six years old at the time of the trial. He was a prominent, seasoned abolitionist attorney and Yale graduate. The script characterizes him as being so desperate to take the case that he stands outside the courthouse and practically assaults Tappan and Joadson. He evidently wears them down in the movie, or they settle for him when Adams initially declines to be involved. In fact, the real abolitionists had an arsenal of attorneys to choose from.

Additionally, the movie depicts tension between Tappan and Baldwin that did not exist. During a meal scene, Baldwin tries to convince Joadson and Tappan that the case is about livestock. Because Baldwin is portrayed as a real estate lawyer, he describes the sale of blacks who were not born in Cuba as being a "wrongful transfer of stolen goods." The cinematic purpose is that the fictionalized Baldwin can undergo a poignant character change when he no longer sees the Africans as chattel, but as human beings. In contrast, the real Baldwin never considered them to be property, much less "stolen goods."

The inaccurate verdict, by the fictitious judge, does not help clarify the legal situation. In the movie, Coglin rejects the salvage claims of Gedney and Meade, contrary to the real facts. He also orders the arrest of Montes and Ruiz on charges of slave trading, a complete concoction. Ruiz and Montes had been arrested earlier, by sheriff's order in New York City. Once they got out of jail, they fled home to Cuba. They were not even in the country when the verdict was read. Nor were the Africans in the courtroom, as depicted in the movie. They were informed of the verdict in jail.

Audiences never learn that Van Buren's administration made secret plans to put the Africans on the USS *Grampus* after Judson's verdict. Adams discussed this example of executive overreaching in the real Supreme Court argument. Certainly, the filmmakers could have incorporated this true instance of executive interference into the movie, instead of injecting it in with the fictional replacement of Coglin for Judson.

While Baldwin tells Cinque in a jail scene that the president has filed an appeal in the Supreme Court, the Africans in the background are jumping around a fire, which they have apparently set. In a book about the *Amistad* mutiny and the movie, a Sierra Leonean scholar contends that this fire dance, "in the confines of a jail . . . makes sense only in light of Western expectations that an African dance around a fire is a necessary ingredient in the definition of Africanness."[23] In the film, when Cinque hears that the case is still ongoing, he feels misled. He decides that he must strip naked in front of the fire to protest the American legal system's inclusion of an appellate process. Furthermore, the movie rewrites procedural rules by allowing the president to bypass an appeal to the circuit court and instead appeal directly to the Supreme Court.

The jurisdiction issue was important in the actual court proceedings. It is only mentioned in the movie when Cinque, through the interpreter Covey, sends questions to Adams as he prepares for the Supreme Court case. Among other questions, Cinque wants to know if Adams has considered the issue of high-seas jurisdiction. Although he responds to one of these suggestions with "good point," Adams eventually gets highly annoyed and shouts, "Now stop this!" Audience members and scholars who are familiar with the real facts might be thinking the same thing themselves. No historical evidence supports the idea that Cinque ever tried giving legal guidance to Adams.

The dramatic highlight of the movie is Adams' Supreme Court argument. His opening sentence is directly from the record: He says that Baldwin argued in so able and complete a manner as to leave him scarcely anything to say. Except for pointing to the Declaration of Independence, the remainder of Adams's speech strays from the true argument. Hopkins, as Adams, takes a

Anthony Hopkins and Djimon Hounsou as Adams and Cinque in front of the U.S. Supreme Court—a scene that never happened in reality.

pill during the oration, perhaps to help swallow all of the inaccuracies that are about to occur. At any rate, Hopkins must be commended for his acting, because even the way he holds his mouth (with the aid of theatrical makeup) precisely replicates photographic images of Adams.

As Adams talks about freedom, dramatic music plays. Cinque, Covey, and Joadson are all fictionally inserted into the courtroom. Adams even makes Cinque stand up because he is "the only true hero in this room." He mentions his greenhouse conversation with his friend Cinque. Cinque and Adams make eye contact to show their connection. Hopkins ambles past busts of former justices and statesmen, and his eyes well up with tears as he makes a speech that Adams never made. Later, Justice Story reads the decision, rendered over one dissent. This is the most accurate verdict of the movie, because it unconditionally freed the Africans. Cinque, who was really in Connecticut at the time, is immediately unchained. The camera focuses on his hands, which he raises in slow motion, literally and figuratively free of the chains.

The movie contains a redeeming, albeit fictional, legal moment. Adams recalls from his days as an attorney that whoever tells the best story wins. Adams describes Joadson's story of being an ex-slave who overcame hardships and devoted his life to the antislavery cause. This does at least personalize the case, reminding the audience that the Africans are individuals, with their own stories, and not just property, as many believed at the time of the *Amistad* case.

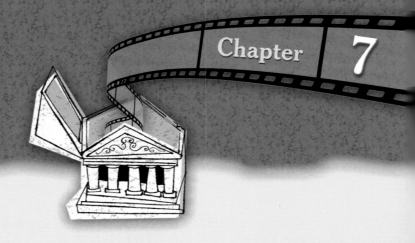

Chapter 7

The Amistad Aftermath

The *Gentleman* anchored at Freetown harbor in mid-January 1842, fifty days after the surviving *Amistad* Africans, interpreter Covey, and the accompanying missionaries set sail. The missionaries faced immediate challenges. They wanted to build a mission station in Cinque's town, but war had destroyed it. Cinque's family was gone, either dead or sold into slavery.

When the missionaries found another location, some of the Mende drifted away. In letters to the United States, missionaries complained of rat-infested conditions and lack of cooperation from the Africans. They also contended with malaria and yellow fever.[1]

Eventually, they set up several missions, naming one of them "Mo Tappan" after Lewis Tappan.[2] One of the girls, Margru, came back to study at Oberlin College in Ohio. She later returned to Africa to teach at the mission.

There are only sketchy accounts about Cinque's life back in Africa. Some reports say, without proof, that he became a slave trader or "reverted to savagery."[3] Others say that he worked as an interpreter at a mission. Many reports claim that he returned to the mission in 1879 to die.

Legal Impact

The two-year-long legal proceedings asserted the power of the United States to rule on an event that occurred on the high seas.[4] A leading *Amistad* scholar describes the case as "the first and only time in history" that "African blacks seized by slave dealers and brought to the New World won their freedom in American courts."[5]

Despite the triumph for Cinque and the other Africans, the Supreme Court's decision was narrow. It did not outlaw slavery. The Court merely recognized that fraud had invalidated the purchase of the recently imported *Amistad* Africans. Notably, the Court acknowledged that if the blacks had been lawfully held as slaves, like Antonio was, then they would have been "merchandise" to be returned under Pinckney's Treaty. Indeed, in subsequent cases, the Supreme Court upheld the right to own slaves.

Related Events

In September 1840, District Attorney William Holabird obtained a court order to sell the *Amistad* and its cargo.

The schooner, in poor condition, was auctioned in October 1840 and sold for $245. The cargo brought in $6,196.14. After the Supreme Court's decision upholding Gedney's salvage award, the case went back to the circuit court to distribute one-third of the total proceeds to Gedney and his crewmates. The Cuban merchants received a small amount. Ruiz and Montes did not receive any payment.

Over the years, the government of Spain continued to seek compensation for the loss of the vessel and cargo. Southerners and subsequent presidential administrations favored Spain's claims, but Congress never approved any award of money to Spain. Once the Civil War ended and slavery was abolished, Spain stopped seeking reimbursement, realizing that its claims were doomed.

Antonio, the slave of the *Amistad*'s slain captain, rethought his original desire to go back to slavery in Cuba. However, Judson had ordered Antonio's surrender to Spain. To help Antonio avoid a return to slavery, Tappan connected Antonio with abolitionists. They moved him secretly to freedom in Canada.

After the Supreme Court triumph, Adams wrote in his diary that despite his physical limitations, his conscience pressed him on to fight for human emancipation.[6] In the House of Representatives, he kept battling the "gag rule," which met its end after nine years in December 1844.

On February 21, 1848, Adams firmly voted "No!" to a resolution to reward veterans of the Mexican War. Abolitionists had opposed the war (1846–1848), viewing it as a means for extending slavery into more regions. Within moments of voting, Adams collapsed on the

Congress floor. Only two days later, Adams died in the Speaker's room.

Roger S. Baldwin became Connecticut's governor in 1844. He advocated giving the right to vote to black citizens and a law to hinder slave-catchers.[7] As a member of the U.S. Senate in 1848, he, like Adams, voted against compensating Spain in the *Amistad* case.[8]

In 1848, Van Buren unsuccessfully ran for president again—this time as a third-party candidate. He was the nominee for the "Free Soil Party," a faction of Democrats who opposed the expansion of slavery into territories. Ironically, his vice-presidential running mate was Charles Francis Adams, Sr., son of John Quincy Adams.

In the twenty years after the *Amistad* Africans returned home, the North and South continued to clash about slavery. Finally, in 1861, the Civil War broke out. Apart from the war, many events during Abraham Lincoln's presidency promoted abolitionism and equal rights. Lincoln tried to reshape the Supreme Court by filling five openings with slavery opponents. Also in his tenure, for the first time since slave trading had been made a capital offense, an American slave ship captain was convicted and executed in 1862. That same year, America, which had withdrawn its naval squadron on the African coast because of the Civil War,

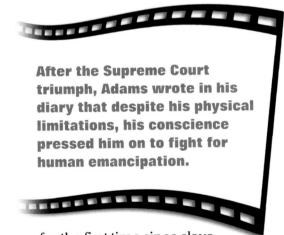

After the Supreme Court triumph, Adams wrote in his diary that despite his physical limitations, his conscience pressed him on to fight for human emancipation.

A replica of the *Amistad*, photographed in New Haven, Connecticut, during a commemoration of the *Amistad* case.

finally granted a mutual limited right of search to British cruisers. This helped to shorten the Atlantic slave trade.

The 1850s was the final decade of significant slave shipping. The last transatlantic slave ship was captured in 1866. By 1869, the West African squadron was not needed.

Lewis Tappan lived to see it all. In January 1863, at seventy-five years old, he cheered the reading of the Emancipation Proclamation at Cooper Hall.[9] In 1865,

Has Slavery Really Been Abolished?

Since World War I, international and regional groups have drafted treaties and declarations against slavery. In 2000, the United Nations adopted the Protocol to Prevent, Suppress and Punish Trafficking in Persons, Especially Women and Children. In 2007, the Justice Department formed a Human Trafficking Prosecution Unit to combat modern day slavery. The American Anti-Slavery Group is a coalition actively working toward abolition. Despite these efforts, slavery continues.

The trafficking of humans is a multi-billion-dollar industry. An estimated twenty-seven million people are enslaved today throughout the world, including between 14,500 to 17,000 victims in the United States.[10] Approximately 1.2 million children are sold into servitude every year, particularly in Asia, Latin America, and Africa.[11]

the Thirteenth Amendment passed, abolishing slavery. Tappan died in 1873.

The end of the Atlantic slave trade did not signify the end of slavery. The trade thrived on the east coast of Africa, and Britain's Royal Navy kept fighting traders for decades.

The *Amistad* Legacy

The *Amistad* case was the impetus for missionary activity in Sierra Leone. The United Brethren in Christ (UBC) eventually assumed responsibility for the Mende Mission. In addition to spreading Christianity, the UBC built many mission schools in Africa, including Harford School for Girls at Moyamba and Albert Academy in Freetown. The first prime minister and the first executive president of Sierra Leone both attended American mission schools and Albert Academy.[12] One of the mission students founded a college that became Florida A & M University in Tallahassee.

The *Amistad* Committee evolved into the American Missionary Association (AMA), the largest abolitionist society in the United States before the Civil War. It developed antislavery churches and publications, and sent missionary agents across the country to preach abolitionism. During and after the war, the AMA educated the freed persons and created more than five hundred schools and colleges in the South. Among the prestigious institutions were Atlanta University, Hampton University, Talladega College, and Fisk University, which have educated many black Americans. Today, it still contributes to some of these colleges.

A three-sided statue of Sengbe Pieh, or Cinque, by Ed Hamilton, stands in front of the city hall of New Haven, Connecticut, the exact site where the captives were held.

Besides supporting the Mende Mission, the AMA established missions for American Indians, fugitive slaves in Canada, Chinese immigrants in California, and other immigrants.[13] The AMA established a Race Relations Department at Fisk University in 1942, which was involved in the civil rights movement. The AMA also founded the Amistad Research Center in 1966. This archives and research library contains volumes of information about the history of minorities in America.

* * *

"We may as well die in trying to be free."—Cinque, before the mutiny on the *Amistad*.

America was helped in the path to abolition because of Cinque's bravery, Tappan's humanitarianism, and Baldwin and Adams's commitment to morality in our legal system. The *Amistad* Africans left an everlasting imprint on the world. The case brought about schools that educated generations of black leaders. One of those men was Martin Luther King, Jr., who, like Cinque, was willing to risk his life for the cause of freedom.

CHAPTER NOTES

1   Cinque's Story

1. "The Long, Low Black Schooner," *Charleston Courier*, September 5, 1839.

2. "The Captured Africans of the Amistad," *New York Morning Herald*, October 4, 1839.

3. New Orleans Times Picayune, October 17, 1839, quoted in, Howard Jones, *Mutiny on the Amistad* (New York: Oxford University Press, 1987), p. 84.

4. Ibid., p. 123.

5. Christopher Martin, *The Amistad Affair* (New York: Abelard-Schuman, 1970), p. 25.

6. Ellen Strong Bartlett, "The *Amistad* Captives," *New England Magazine*, March 1900, p. 72.

7. Captain Theophilus Conneau, *A Slaver's Log Book or 20 Years' Residence in Africa* (Englewood Cliffs, N.J.: Prentice-Hall, 1976), p. 55.

8. Howard Thomas, ed., *Black Voyage: Eyewitness Accounts of the Atlantic Slave Trade* (Boston: Little, Brown and Company, 1971), p. 90.

9. Daniel Mannix, *Black Cargoes: A History of the Atlantic Slave Trade, 1518–1865* (New York: Viking Press, 1962), p. 104.

10. Thomas, p. 93.

11. Mannix, p. 111.

12. Martin, p. 30.

13. John Reader, *Africa: A Biography of the Continent* (New York: Alfred A. Knopf, 1999), p. 390.

14. Howard Jones, *Mutiny on the* Amistad (New York: Oxford University Press, 1987), p. 15.

15. Steven M. Wise, *Though the Heavens May Fall: The Landmark Trial That Led to the End of Human Slavery* (Cambridge, Mass.: De Capo Press, 2005), p. 2; W. E. F. Ward, *The Royal Navy and the Slavers: The Suppression of the Atlantic Slave Trade* (New York: Pantheon Books, 1969), p. 33.

16. Ward, p. 33.

17. Mannix, p. 120.

18. Jones, p. 16.

19. Conneau, p. 71.

20. Ibid.

21. Ibid., p. 72.

22. Martin, p. 32.

23. Edward Guthmann, "Middling Passage: Sentiment threatens to sink Spielberg's earnest slave-revolt epic, 'Amistad,'" *SFGate*, December 12, 1997, <www.sfgate.com/cgi-bin/article.cgi?f=/c/a/1997/12/12/DD55150.DTL> (January 14, 2009).

24. "Movie Reviews of Amistad: The New Republic, Stanley Kaufmann, December 22, 1997," Famous American Trials Web page: Amistad Trials, 1839–1840, 1998, <http://www.law.umkc.edu/faculty/projects/ftrials/amistad/AMI_MOVI.HTM#Reviews> (January 14, 2009).

25. Simeon Baldwin, "The Captives of the *Amistad*," A Paper Read Before the New Haven Colony Historical Society, 1886, p. 332, <http://digital.lib.msu.edu/collections/index.cfm?TitleID=248> (November 22, 2006).

 The Mutiny

1. Howard Jones, *Mutiny on the* Amistad (New York: Oxford University Press, 1987), p. 24.

2. Doug Linder, "Stamped With Glory: Lewis Tappan and the Africans of the *Amistad*," 2000, <http://www.law.umkc.edu/faculty/projects/ftrials/trialheroes/Tappanessay.html> (October 6, 2006).

3. Simeon Baldwin, "The Captives of the *Amistad*," A Paper Read Before the New Haven Colony Historical Society, 1886, p. 333, <digital.lib.msu.edu/collections> (November 22, 2006).

4. Jones, pp. 24–28.
5. "The Long, Low, Black Schooner," *Charleston Courier*, September 5, 1839.
6. "Supposed Pirate," *New Orleans Bee*, September 4, 1839.
7. "Weird Ship," *Richmond Enquirer*, August 30, 1839.
8. "The Long, Low Black Schooner," *Charleston Courier*, September 5, 1839.
9. Ibid.; "Suspicious Schooner," *Richmond Enquirer*, September 6, 1839, p. 4.
10. "Weird Ship," *Richmond Enquirer*, August 30, 1839.
11. "Supposed Pirate," *New Orleans Bee*, September 4, 1839.
12. Ibid.
13. Mary Cable, *Black Odyssey: The Case of the Slave Ship "Amistad"* (Viking Press: New York, 1971), p. 4.
14. Ibid.
15. "The Spanish Slaver," *New York Morning Herald*, August 26, 1839.
16. "The Long, Low, Black Schooner," *Charleston Courier*, September 5, 1839.
17. Baldwin, p. 334.
18. "Testimony of Henry Green, U.S. District Court, Connecticut, November 19, 1839," Exploring *Amistad* at Mystic Seaport, n.d., <amistad.mysticseaport.org/library/court/district/1839.11.19.greentest.html> (February 26, 2007).
19. Ibid.; Jones, p. 28.

 Abolitionists Unite

1. Don Jordan and Michael Walsh, *White Cargo: History of Britain's White Slaves in America* (New York: New York University Press, 2008), p. 12.
2. David Brion Davis, *Inhuman Bondage: The Rise and Fall of Slavery in the New World* (New York: Oxford University Press, 2006), pp. 132–33.
3. W.E.F. Ward, *The Royal Navy and the Slavers: The Suppression of the Atlantic Slave Trade* (New York: Pantheon Books, 1969), p. 87.

4. Ibid.

5. Hugh Thomas, *The Slave Trade* (New York: Simon & Schuster, 1997), p. 566.

6. Daniel Mannix, *Black Cargoes: A History of the Atlantic Slave Trade, 1518–1865* (New York: Viking Press, 1962), p. 210.

7. Thomas, p. 662.

8. Mannix, p. 208.

9. Ibid.

10. Davis, p. 257.

11. Ibid., p. 256.

12. Bruce Levine, *Half Slave and Half Free: The Roots of Civil War* (New York: Hill and Wang, 1992), p. 153.

13. William Lee Miller, *Arguing About Slavery* (New York: Alfred A. Knopf, 1996), p. 97.

14. Ibid., p. 11.

15. Ibid.

16. Horatio Strother, *The Underground Railroad in Connecticut* (Middletown, Conn.: Wesleyan University Press, 1962), p. 83.

17. Jones, p. 228, n. 27.

18. Frank G. Kirkpatrick, "Religious Abolitionists in the *Amistad* Era: Diversity in Moral Discourse," *The Connecticut Scholar: Occasional Papers of the Connecticut Humanities Council*, 1992, no. 10: pp. 44–63, <http://amistad.mysticseaport.org/discovery/themes/connscholar.92/kirkpatrick.abolition.html> (December 7, 2006).

19. Ibid.

4 The Legal Fight for Freedom

1. "Suspicious Schooner," *Richmond Enquirer*, September 6, 1839, p. 4; "The Case of the Captured Negroes," *New York Morning Herald*, September 9, 1839.

2. "Amistad Case as Revolution," *Colored American*, October 5, 1839; and "On Cinques," *Colored American*, October 19, 1839, p. 1.

3. Arthur Abraham, "The Amistad Revolt: An Historical Legacy of Sierra Leone and the United States," n.d., <usa.us embassy.de/etexts/soc/amistad.pdf> (January 14, 2009).

4. "The Africans," *New York Commercial Advertiser*, October 8, 1839.

5. Simeon Baldwin, "The Captives of the *Amistad*," A Paper Read Before the New Haven Colony Historical Society, 1886, p. 343, <digital.lib.msu.edu/collections> (November 22, 2006).

6. Ibid., p. 342.

7. Howard Jones, *Mutiny on the* Amistad (New York: Oxford University Press, 1987), p. 52.

8. Ibid.

9. *The Amistad Revolt: All We Want is Make Us Free*, The Amistad Committee (video), New Haven, CT, 1995; Diana R. McCain, "Free Men: The *Amistad* Revolt and the American Antislavery Movement," pp. 3–4.

10. Howard Jones, "Mutiny on the *Amistad*: All We Want is Make Us Free," *The Connecticut Scholar: Occasional Papers of the Connecticut Humanities Council, 1992*, no. 10, pp. 7–25, <http://amistad.mysticseaport.org/discovery/themes/conn scholar.92/jones.mutiny.html> (October 28, 2008).

11. Lewis Tappan, *African Captives: Trial of the Prisoners of the Amistad on the Writ of Habeas Corpus, Before the Circuit Court of the United States, For the District of Connecticut, at Hartford; Judges Thompson and Judson, September Term, 1839* (New York: American Antislavery Society, 1839), p. 9.

12. Horatio Strother, *The Underground Railroad in Connecticut* (Middletown, Conn.: Wesleyan University Press, 1962), p. 111.

13. Tappan, p. 46.

14. Bernard C. Steiner, *History of Slavery in Connecticut* (Baltimore: Johns Hopkins University Press, 1893), p. 49, <http://www.dinsdoc.com/steiner-2_2.htm> (December 7, 2006). For a summary of the facts in the Prudence Crandall case, see Steiner, pp. 45–52.

15. Jones, *Mutiny on the* Amistad, p. 97.

16. Steiner, p. 52.

17. Ellen Strong Bartlett, "The *Amistad* Captives," *New England Magazine*, March 1900, p. 78.

18. Ibid., pp. 78–79.

19. Doug Linder, "Stamped With Glory: Lewis Tappan and the Africans of the *Amistad*," p. 18, 2000, <www.law.umkc.edu/faculty/projects/ftrials/trialheroes/Tappanessay.html> (October 6, 2006).

20. Ibid.

21. Baldwin, p. 346.

22. Madden deposition, U.S. District Court Records for Connecticut, Federal Archives and Records Center, Waltham, Mass., November 20, 1839, <www.law.umkc.edu/faculty/projects/ftrials/amistad/AMI_TMAD.HTM> (October 10, 2006).

23. Jones, p. 121.

24. Ibid., p. 241, n. 21.

25. "Testimony of Professor Josiah W. Gibbs, January 8, 1840, U.S. District Court, Connecticut," Exploring *Amistad* at Mystic Seaport, n.d., <amistad.mysticseaport.org/library.court/district/1840.1.8.gibbstest.html?frames=on> (February 26, 2007).

26. John Barber, "A History of the *Amistad* Captives" (New Haven, Conn.: E.L. and J.W. Barber, 1840), p. 52.

27. Tappan, p. 14.

28. "The Africans," *New York Commercial Advertiser*, October 8, 1839.

29. Foster Wild Rice, "Nathaniel Jocelyn 1796–1881," *Connecticut Historical Society Bulletin*, vol. 31, no. 4, October 1996, p. 102.

30. Barber, p. 53.

31. Howard Jones, "Mutiny on the *Amistad*: All We Want is Make Us Free," *The Connecticut Scholar*: Occasional Papers of the Connecticut Humanities Council, 1992, no. 10, pp. 7–25.

32. "Testimony of Grabeau, January 8, 1840, U.S. District Court, Connecticut," Exploring *Amistad* at Mystic Seaport, n.d., <http://amistad.mysticseaport.org/library/court/district/1840.1.8.grabeautest.html?frames=on> (February 26, 2007); "Testimony of Fuliwa, January 8, 1840, U.S. District Court, Connecticut," Exploring *Amistad* at Mystic Seaport, n.d.,

<http://amistad.mysticseaport.org/library/court/district/1840. 1.8.fuliwatest.html?frames=on> (February 26, 2007).

33. Jones, *Mutiny on the* Amistad, pp. 126–27.

34. "Statement of A. G. Vega, Spanish Consul," Famous American Trials Web page: Amistad Trials, 1839–1840, 1998, <www.law.umkc.edu/faculty/projects/ftrials/amistad/AMI_ TVEG.HTM> (October 10, 2006).

35. "*Amistad* Case—Proceedings of Friday," *New York Journal of Commerce*, January 13, 1840.

36. Barber, p. 54

37. Ibid., p. 55; Jones, *Mutiny on the* Amistad, p. 128.

38. Barber, p. 54.

39. Ibid.

40. "*Amistad* Case—Proceedings of Friday," *New York Journal of Commerce*, January 13, 1840.

41. Barber, p. 61.

 ## The Final Legal Battle

1. Simeon Baldwin, "The Captives of the *Amistad*," A Paper Read Before the New Haven Colony Historical Society, 1886, p. 348, <digital.lib.msu.edu/collections> (November 22, 2006).

2. Howard Jones, *Mutiny on the* Amistad (New York: Oxford University Press, 1987), pp. 133–134.

3. Ibid., p. 133.

4. Ibid., pp. 152–153.

5. William Lee Miller, *Arguing About Slavery* (New York: Alfred A. Knopf, 1996), p. 187.

6. Baldwin, p. 346.

7. Bernard C. Steiner, *History of Slavery in Connecticut* (Baltimore: Johns Hopkins University Press, 1893), p. 63.

8. Jack Shepherd, *The Adams Chronicles: Four Generations of Greatness* (Boston: Little, Brown and Company, 1975), p. 333.

9. Doug Linder, "Stamped With Glory: Lewis Tappan and the Africans of the *Amistad*," p. 13, 2000, <www.law.umkc.

edu/faculty/projects/ftrials.trialheroes/Tappanessay.html> (October 6, 2006).

10. Miller, p. 166.

11. Ibid., p. 400.

12. Arthur Abraham, "The Amistad Revolt: An Historical Legacy of Sierra Leone and the United States," n.d., <usa.us embassy.de/etexts/soc/amistad.pdf> (January 14, 2009).

13. Supreme Court Rules 28.3 and 28.4.

14. Peter Irons, *A People's History of the Supreme Court* (New York: Viking, 1999), p. 147.

15. Jones, p. 188.

16. James McClellan, *Joseph Story and the American Constitution* (Norman, Okla.: University of Oklahoma Press, 1971), p. 297.

17. Joseph Wheelan, *Mr. Adams's Last Crusade* (New York: Public Affairs, 2008), p. 177.

18. Charles Warren, *The Supreme Court in United States History: Vol. Two, 1836–1918* (Boston: Little, Brown and Company, 1922), p. 74.

19. Allan Nevins, ed., *The Diary of John Quincy Adams 1994–1845* (New York: Frederick Ungar Publishing Co., 1969), p. 518.

20. "Argument of John Quincy Adams for the Appellees," Famous American Trials Web page: Amistad Trials, 1839–1840, 1998, <www.law.umkc.edu/faculty/projects/ftrials/amistad/adamsarg.html> (December 22, 2006).

21. Ibid.

22. Warren, p. 76.

23. Miller, p. 402.

24. Strother, p. 78.

25. Jones, pp. 204–205.

26. Linder, p. 14.

27. David Brion Davis, *Inhuman Bondage: The Rise and Fall of Slavery in the New World* (New York: Oxford University Press, 2006), p. 24.

28. Linder, p. 15.

Amistad: The Movie

1. Donald Dale Jackson, "Mutiny on the *Amistad*," *Smithsonian*, vol. 28, no. 9, December 1997.

2. Rita Kempley, " 'Amistad': History Unshackled," *Washington Post*, December 12, 1997.

3. Evelyn Jamilah, "History as told by . . . Professor Proclaims His Amistad Ancestry," *Black Issues in Higher Education*, vol. 14, no. 25, February 5, 1998, p. 24.

4. Richard Alleva, "Amistad and Titanic," *Commonweal*, February 13, 1998, <http://www.findarticles.com/p/articles/ mi_m1252/is_n3_v125/ai_20463664> (November 22, 2006); Emanuel Levy and Elizabeth Guider, "Amistad," *Variety.com*, December 1, 1997, <www.variety.com/review/VE111711764? categoryid=31&cs=1&s=h&p=0> (October 1, 2008).

5. Alleva; Russell Smith, "Amistad," *Austin Chronicle*, December 19, 1997.

6. Levy and Guider.

7. Roger Ebert, "Amistad," *Chicago Sun-Times*, December 12, 1997, <rogerebert.suntimes.com/apps/pbcs.dll/article?AID +/19971212/REVIEWS/712120301/1023> (October 1, 2008).

8. Iyunolu Folayan Osagie, *The Amistad Revolt: Memory, Slavery, and the Politics of Identity in the United States and Sierra Leone* (Athens, Ga.: University of Georgia Press, 2000), p. 127.

9. John Woolard, "When Steven Spielberg Was Looking for a Slave Ship, the Long Beach-Based Nautical Heritage Society Had Just the Vessel," *Long Beach Press Telegram*, December 13, 1997.

10. James Berardelli, "Amistad: A Film Review," n.d., <www.reel reviews.net/movies/a/amistad.html> (October 7, 2006).

11. Ibid.

12. Doug Linder, "Salvaging Amistad," *Journal of Maritime Law and Commerce*, vol. 31, no. 4, October 2000, <www.law. umkc.edu/faculty/projects/ftrials/amistad/Salvaging.html> (October 6, 2006).

13. Osagie, p. 122.

14. William A. Owens, *Black Mutiny: The Revolt on the Schooner Amistad* (New York: Penguin Putnam, 1997).

15. Osagie, p. 126.

16. Ibid., p. 127; Eric Foner, "The *Amistad* Case in Fact and Film," March 1998, <http://historymatters.gmu.edu/d/74> (July 5, 2008).

17. Robert L. Paquette, "From History to Hollywood: The Voyage of 'La Amistad,'" *The New Criterion*, 2008, <www.new criterion.com/articles.cfm/amistad-paquette-3100> (October 28, 2008).

18. Linder.

19. Sally Hadden, "Amistad," History Department, Florida State University, Published by H-Law, December 1997, <www. h-net.org/mmreviews/showrev.cgi?path=49> (October 10, 2006).

20. Paquette.

21. Ibid.

22. Osagie, p. 121.

23. Ibid., p. 30.

7   The *Amistad* Aftermath

1. Douglas O. Linder, "The *Amistad* Case," <www.law.umkc. edu/faculty/projects/ftrials/amistad/AMI_ACT.HTM> (February 26, 2007).

2. Arthur Abraham, "The *Amistad* Revolt: An Historical Legacy of Sierra Leone and the United States," n.d., <usa.us embassy.de/etexts/soc/amistad.pdf> (January 14, 2009).

3. Simeon Baldwin, "The Captives of the *Amistad*," A Paper Read Before the New Haven Colony Historical Society, 1886, p. 364 (citing New Haven *Daily Palladium*, January 13, 1840) <digital.lib.msu.edu/collections> (November 22, 2006).

4. Denise Barnes, "Hollywood's Color Barrier—Critics Debate the Merits of Making the Film *Amistad* by a White Director," *Insight on the News*, March 2, 1998, <www.findarticles.com /p/articles/mi_m1571/is_n8_v14/ai_20351802> (November 10, 2006).

5. Howard Jones, *American History*, January/February 1998, <www.historynet.com/culture/african_american_history/3031201.html?showAll=y&c=y> (March 8, 2007).

6. Allan Nevins, ed., *The Diary of John Quincy Adams 1994–1845* (New York: Frederick Ungar Publishing Co., 1969), p. 519.

7. Horatio Strother, *The Underground Railroad in Connecticut* (Middletown, Conn.: Wesleyan University Press, 1962), p. 81.

8. Ibid.

9. Doug Linder, "Stamped With Glory: Lewis Tappan and the Africans of the *Amistad*," 2000, p. 19, <www.law.umkc.edu/faculty/projects/ftrials.trialheroes/Tappanessay.html> (October 6, 2006).

10. "Modern Slavery 101," iAbolish: American Anti-Slavery Group, n.d., <www.iabolish.org/modern_slavery101> (March 15, 2007).

11. Sharon LaFraniere, "Africa's World of Forced Labor, in a 6-Year-Old's Eyes," *New York Times*, Oct. 29, 2006, p. 16; Francis Bok, *Escape From Slavery: The True Story of My Ten Years in Captivity—and My Journey to Freedom in America* (New York: St. Martin's Press, 2003).

12. Abraham, pp. 45–46.

13. Clifton H. Johnson, "The *Amistad* Case and Its Consequences in U.S. History," reprinted in "The Amistad Story," a publication of the New Haven Colony Historical Society, p. 20.

GLOSSARY

abolitionists—People who actively work toward ending slavery.

admiralty law—Also known as "maritime law," the rules governing ships on the high seas.

appeal—To challenge a lower court's decision by requesting review from a higher court.

colonization—A movement in the 1800s to transport freed African Americans on a voluntary basis to Liberia, an area without slavery on the west coast of Africa.

cross-examination—The questioning of a witness by the lawyer for the party who is opposed to that witness.

deposition—The taking of a witness's oral or written testimony, under oath, outside of the courtroom before the trial.

direct examination—The questioning of a witness by the lawyer who is offering the testimony of that witness.

emancipation—Freeing people from slavery.

gradualism—The belief that slavery should be phased out slowly.

grand jury—A group that hears evidence and makes factual findings, including the decision of whether a person should be formally charged with a crime.

habeas corpus—Latin for "you should have the body," it is a legal protection from unlawful imprisonment by the government.

immediatists—People who believed that slavery should end as soon as possible.

jurisdiction—A court's power to hear a certain case, based on the court's authority to handle the subject matter of the case or on the crime's location.

Pinckney's Treaty—A commercial pact between the United States and Spain in 1795, renewed in 1819 as the Adams-Onís Treaty, that required nations to restore to the owners "all ships and merchandise" rescued from pirates or robbers at the high seas.

salvage—In admiralty law, a reward for assisting other vessels that are in trouble at sea, calculated as a percentage of the ship and its cargo.

FURTHER READING

Books

DeFord, Deborah H. *Life Under Slavery.* Philadelphia: Chelsea House Publishers, 2006.

Doak, Robin Santos. *Slave Rebellions.* New York: Facts on File, 2006.

Gold, Susan Dudley. *United States v. Amistad: Slave Ship Mutiny.* Tarrytown, N.Y.: Marshall Cavendish Benchmark, 2006.

Hulm, David. *United States v. The Amistad: The Question of Slavery in a Free Country.* New York: Rosen Publishing Group, 2004.

Lester, Julius. *To Be a Slave.* New York: Dial Books, 1998.

McKissack, Patricia C., and Fredrick L. McKissack. *Rebels Against Slavery: American Slave Revolts.* New York: Scholastic, 2006.

Myers, Walter Dean. *Amistad: A Long Road to Freedom.* New York: Puffin Books, 2001.

Watkins, Richard. *Slavery: Bondage Throughout History.* Boston: Houghton Mifflin, 2001.

Internet Addresses

Amistad Trial Page
<http://www.law.umkc.edu/faculty/projects/ftrials/amistad/AMISTD.htm>

Federal Judicial Center
<http://www.fjc.gov/history/amistad.nsf/page/cinque>

Mystic Seaport
<http://amistad.mysticseaport.org>

ACKNOWLEDGMENTS

The author thanks the following people for their insights and help: Alfred L. Marder, President of the Amistad Committee, Inc., in New Haven, Connecticut; James W. Campbell, Librarian and Curator of Manuscripts at the New Haven Colony Historical Society; Joanie Gearin, Archivist at National Archives and Records Administration—Northeast Region in Waltham, Massachusetts; Barbara Austen, Manuscript Archivist/Cataloger at the Connecticut Historical Society Museum in Hartford; Cynthia Harbeson, Reference Librarian and Assistant Archivist at the Connecticut Historical Society. The author also thanks her in-laws, Harry and Rose Azarian, for being so supportive. She is especially grateful to her husband, Phil Azarian, for his knowledge of nautical history, and their children, Samantha and Alex, for their patience during this project.

INDEX